Experimental Research Methods in Sociolinguistics

Other titles in the Research Methods in Linguistics series

Experimental Research Methods in Language Learning, AekPhakiti

Quantitative Research in Linguistics, 2nd edition, Sebastian Rasinger

Research Methods in Applied Linguistics, edited by Brian Paltridge and
   AekPhakiti

Research Methods in Interpreting, Sandra Hale and Jemina Napier

Research Methods in Linguistics, LiaLitosseliti

Experimental Research Methods in Sociolinguistics

Katie Drager

Bloomsbury Academic
An imprint of Bloomsbury Publishing Plc

B L O O M S B U R Y
LONDON · OXFORD · NEW YORK · NEW DELHI · SYDNEY

Bloomsbury Academic

An imprint of Bloomsbury Publishing Plc

50 Bedford Square	1385 Broadway
London	New York
WC1B 3DP	NY 10018
UK	USA

www.bloomsbury.com

BLOOMSBURY and the Diana logo are trademarks of Bloomsbury Publishing Plc

First published 2018

British Library Cataloguing-in-Publication Data
A catalogue record for this book is available from the British Library.

ISBN: HB: 978-1-4742-5177-8
PB: 978-1-4742-5178-5
ePDF: 978-1-4742-5180-8
ePub: 978-1-4742-5179-2

Library of Congress Cataloging-in-Publication Data
A catalog record for this book is available from the Library of Congress.

Cover image © Getty Images/DrAfter123

Series: Research Methods in Linguistics

Typeset by Newgen KnowledgeWorks Pvt. Ltd., Chennai, India
Printed and bound in Great Britain

To find out more about our authors and books visit www.bloomsbury.com. Here you will find extracts, author interviews, details of forthcoming events and the option to sign up for our newsletters.

To

Jen Hay

Contents

Illustrations

Tables

Acknowledgments

As with many endeavors as large as writing a book, there are many people who contributed in a variety of different ways. First and foremost, I would like to thank Jen Hay, to whom this book is dedicated. Jen was my advisor during both my M.A. and Ph.D., and she taught me much of what I know about experimental design. But her role in my professional life has been much greater than that. Jen is inspiring and patient and kind, and she believed in me at a time in my life when I didn't believe in myself and for that I am eternally grateful.

I am also grateful to Amy Schafer, who taught me everything I know about eye-tracking, and Abby Walker who gets as excited as I do about cool new research ideas. I am also grateful to the feedback I received from James Grama and Anna Belew on earlier versions of some chapters, and to ʻŌiwiHawaiʻiokalani Parker Jones for his feedback on the section on EEG/ERP in Chapter 5. I am extremely grateful to all of the scholars who agreed to share their experiment materials on the companion website; I hope you all find them as helpful as I have.

On a more personal note, I am grateful to my son, Alapaʻi, for forcing me to take much-needed breaks, and for the unborn baby in my belly who – while making it more difficult to write the book – didn't make it impossible. Finally, I want to thank my husband, Keola Jarrett, whose support throughout the process of writing this book has been unwavering. While writing, I often find myself thinking about all of the women scholars and academic mamas who came before me and helped pave the way; it was not so long ago that a pregnant academic mother would not have produced this book. The vast majority of whatever success I've achieved is a direct result of the people I've had around me and the people who came before me, and I am grateful to all of them, whether I know them personally or not.

Introduction

This book is intended for readers who are unfamiliar with experimental methods but who are at least vaguely interested in using them. I hope that it will inspire new research and courses in experimental sociolinguistics, but it should also be helpful to anyone who just wants to decode what experimenters are talking about when they present their work (e.g., *What in the world does it mean when someone says that the stimuli are counterbalanced? What's the difference between controlling and balancing a variable?*). I hope that you, the reader, find this book useful and that it piques your interest in the methods and the types of questions they can be used to address.

This book is written primarily as a tool to assist you with the research that you want to conduct, assuming that you don't already have the necessary training or that there are gaps in your knowledge regarding experimental methods. The style is informal and conversational (this is my preferred teaching style), so I've avoided fancypants words in favor of keeping the explanations simple and easy to understand. When jargon is necessary (or, at least, important for you to know and use if you are going to write and publish experimental work), I define it in textboxes that are separated from the main text. At the end of every chapter is a summary of main points and a list of suggested readings that can offer further guidance on experimental methods.

For each chapter, there is also a corresponding page on the companion website. On the website, you will find materials, such as stimuli and scripts used for data collection and analysis, from some of the experiments discussed in the book. You are encouraged to browse these resources and use them for teaching and learning the methods. However, if you would like to use any of the materials in your own work (e.g., repurpose stimuli to replicate an experiment), please request permission from the author(s) of the work.

It is worth noting that many methods commonly used in sociolinguistics are not discussed in this book, including many that are quantitative. For example, this book only briefly discusses the best practices of designing and conducting surveys (such as those that look at intergenerational transmission or language attitudes) and the types of map tasks that are used to study folk linguistic impressions of dialects. While these are certainly useful tools for sociolinguists and I've used them in my own work, they are not covered in this book because they are not strictly experimental. Furthermore, they are discussed in detail elsewhere (e.g., Mallinson, Childs, & Herk 2013) and, quite frankly, the book would simply be too large and unwieldy were I to try and cover every single method used by sociolinguists.

What is covered is a range of different experimental paradigms as well as descriptions of what are currently considered to be the best practices when employing them. I cover methodologies for looking at speech production, perception, and language ideologies, from those that are designed to examine more naturalistic speech data to those that are highly controlled. Different experimental paradigms and equipment are recommended depending on the specific research situation; for example, if the researcher is working with an endangered language, they may have different considerations (e.g., remoteness of field site; number of possible participants) than a researcher conducting lab-based work with a widely spoken language. The book is written taking into consideration the different approaches that would be appropriate for different cultures, languages, writing systems, and research goals and, as such, it is intended to be a general introduction to experimental methods for a wide range of researchers interested in the topic.

While the book is aimed primarily at sociolinguists, researchers from other areas such as Laboratory Phonology, Social Psychology, First and Second Language Acquisition, and Psycholinguistics may find the book helpful, as these are areas that have informed much of the work in Experimental Sociolinguistics.

The book has seven chapters. Chapter 1 introduces you to the many different kinds of sociolinguistic research questions that experimental methods can be used to answer. It begins by discussing what we mean by *experiment* (it's not as straightforward as you might think) and then delves into the different research questions, such as: What social meanings are associated with a particular dialect? And what factors influence whether someone converges on the speech of an interlocutor? Examples of research that addresses the questions are provided to give you an idea of papers you should read if you are interested in conducting work along these lines. Hopefully by the end of Chapter 1, you will be convinced that experiments are useful tools for sociolinguists.

In Chapter 2, you are introduced to the practicalities of running an experiment, from recording auditory stimuli to recruiting participants to making methodological decisions that fit the needs of the particular speech community you're working with. The challenges, drawbacks, and advantages to different methodological decisions are presented alongside a discussion of how to create good, controlled stimuli. Also discussed are the reasons why it's important to randomize stimuli and the different possible technologies that can be used for data collection. You will be directed to other resources (e.g., Praat scripts for vowel resynthesis) so that you can learn about those techniques should they be necessary for your interests. Also discussed are ethics in experimental work and some benefits and challenges of publishing work in Experimental Sociolinguistics.

Chapters 3, 4, and 5 focus on experimental design: Chapter 3 focuses on experimental paradigms used to look at speech perception and Chapter 4 focuses on those used to look at speech production. Example experiments (ones that have not been conducted but I think would be interesting for someone to do) are provided in both chapters. Chapter 5 introduces the reader to experimental methods that are rarely used in sociolinguistics but that present some exciting possibilities for future research. Most of these methods require a large amount of training (far beyond what I can offer in this text) as well as specialized equipment that can be very expensive to acquire. Therefore, I have included only relatively brief descriptions of the methods, including some reasons why you should seek further training before attempting them.

The main goals of Chapter 6 are to help you determine the best way to visualize your data and test the significance of any patterns you observe. In order to achieve this goal, I discuss setting up spreadsheets and I introduce you to R. Through reading this chapter and working through the associated R script and sample dataset (both available on the companion website), you will learn some R basics as well as how to produce graphs and run statistics. There are entire books on this subject (some of which are very good and are recommended as further reading), so this chapter serves merely as an introduction to the kinds of statistical tests that are commonly used.

Chapter 7 provides some final thoughts on experimental methods in sociolinguistics while addressing some final questions you may have about conducting experimental work.

Defining and constraining the research question

1

Having identified something
that might be of interest for sociolinguistic study,
the first step is to decide precisely
what is potentially interesting about it.
This involves articulating half-formed hunches
into clear, answerable questions.

– Barbara Johnstone (2000: 4)

1.1. What is an experiment?

Before we dive into specifics on conducting experiments, it's important to first understand what the word *experiment* means. For many people, the word invokes images of white coats and invasive procedures. However, most experiments (and certainly those within sociolinguistics) are minimally invasive; people who take part in an experiment might read some sentences, talk with an experimenter, and/or use a mouse to click on a picture. Furthermore, while many experiments are conducted in labs, others are conducted in workplaces, urban apartment buildings, or homes in rural villages.

The *Oxford English Dictionary* defines an experiment as "an action or operation undertaken in order to discover something unknown, to test a hypothesis, or establish or illustrate some known truth" (*OED*). Under this definition, experiments include just about anything that is research-related. However, in this book, I use a narrower definition, one that is used by social scientists: experiments are tasks that follow the **experimental method**. In the experimental method, the researcher manipulates a factor (known as the **independent variable**) that is hypothesized to have an effect on some variable outcome (known as the **dependent variable**). The manipulation is done to identify cause and effect, testing what factor or factors have an effect on behavior. Thus, while many people conflate quantitative and experimental methods, producing quantitative data is not enough to make a technique experimental (correlation does not equal causation and it is causation that experiments aim to investigate), and not all experimental data are quantitative (see e.g., the part of Section 2.1.2 that discusses open-ended questions).

What's that?

An **experiment** is a type of research method that uses the experimental method in order to test the effect of a factor on some variable.

The **experimental method** is the practice of manipulating a factor in order to test its effect on a variable outcome.

The **dependent variable** is the outcome factor being tested.

Independent variables are the factors that are hypothesized to have some influence on the dependent variable.

The **conditions** in an experiment are the variants of the independent variable under hypothesis.

Examples of manipulated and dependent variables are shown in Table 1.1. The different versions of the manipulated factor are called **conditions**. When experiments are set up properly, a difference in the dependent variable across conditions provides evidence that the conditions influence the dependent variable.

Table 1.1 Overview of dependent variables in select sociolinguistic experiments

Study	Dependent variables	Independent variables (i.e., testing effect of X)	Conditions
Labov & Ash (1997)	accuracy	talker's regional dialect	talker dialects
Most et al. (2007)	reaction time	talker's gender & gender associated with the word	male & female talkers
Pantos & Perkins (2012)	reaction time	talker's accent	L1 & L2 speakers
Squires (2013a)	interpretation	sentence structure of prime	standard & non-standard constructions
Pharao et al. (2014)	rating	talker's style	modern & street styles
McGowan (2015)	accuracy of transcription	ethnicity of person in image	Chinese & Caucasian faces
Hay et al. (2009)	degree of merger	experimenter identity	NZ & US experimenters
Kim et al. (2011)	perceived similarity	dialect of speakers	L1 & L2 speakers

The idea is that – assuming all else is the same across conditions – we can conclude that the condition had an effect on the dependent variable if the dependent variable is found to vary across conditions. The assumption that all else is the same relies on there being a great deal of control over other factors that could potentially influence the dependent variable. (Control is a concept I will come back to over and over again throughout this book.) However, despite our best efforts to control everything possible, we constantly break the assumption that everything is equal across conditions. For example, we might compare responses from different subjects across conditions (subjects ≠ equal), the questions might be shown in a random order (order ≠ equal), the day or time of day that the experiment was run might be different (date ≠ equal), or the experimenter might be wearing different clothes or have a different hairstyle (hair brushed ≠ equal). We do our best to control everything possible and (especially) anything that we hypothesize might influence the dependent variable. But while it may seem unlikely that, say, time of day influences whether a stimulus is perceived as *pin* or *pen*, it's still possible. Because of this (and because it's normally unrealistic to test all possible subjects or all possible contexts), we work with likelihoods instead of absolute certainties. Therefore, when we frame our results, we say things like "The results provide evidence that…" instead of stronger claims like "The results prove…" The more independent studies that provide evidence in support of some hypothesis, the more confident we become that the hypothesis is true. This is why replication is so important. (See Section 7.1 for further discussion of replication along with a call for journals, editors, and reviewers to support publication of replicated studies.) Quantitative data include anything analyzed in terms of numbers, such as counts, ranges, or proportions. This contrasts with qualitative data, which are descriptive without being numeric. Some methods, such as surveys, can be used to produce both types of data. Included in this book are several tasks that produce qualitative rather than quantitative results or, in other cases, they produce quantitative data that are not appropriate for statistical analysis. However, the majority of methods covered in this book are quantitative since most experiments produce quantitative data.

Usually, we refer to people who take part in experiments as **participants**, **subjects**, or (for work on spoken languages) **speakers** or **listeners**. The objects that are used to cause some effect on the behavior of the participants are called **stimuli**. Stimuli can be anything from sentences to photographs to beer; it really all depends on what experimental paradigm you're using and what specific research question you're testing. (A wide range of possible experimental paradigms to choose from are presented in Chapters 3, 4, and 5.) When voices are used as stimuli, the person associated with a voice is often referred to as a **talker** in the text reporting the results, differentiating talkers from any speakers who are participants.

Experiments are a powerful method of data collection because they provide a means to control for things that you wouldn't otherwise be able to control for. For example, experiments can ensure that you get enough tokens of a variable of interest and that you have equal numbers of tokens across the different participants (i.e., controlling for number of test items). Other variables that influence the variable of interest will also be controlled or balanced in a well-designed experiment. These other variables include social factors, like social characteristics attributed to an addressee, and linguistic factors that are less social in nature, such as the surrounding phonological environment or a token's prosodic structure.

If we **control** a variable, it means that we hold it constant (e.g., the addressee is always the same person). In contrast, when we **balance** a variable, it means that there are equal numbers of the different variants of that variable (e.g., there are two addressees with an equal number of participants interacting with each). So, for example, if I'm running an experiment testing the effect of a talker's emotion (e.g., happy vs. sad) on the perception of a vowel, I need to balance the different phonological environments that influence that vowel's realization, making sure that there are an equal number of items in each environment and that the environments are evenly distributed across conditions. Likewise, if my stimulus sentences have two different prosodies, all combinations of the different phonological environments need to be found with each prosody, in equal numbers. We call this **balancing across cells**. But during the design process, I might find that balancing the factors results in an unreasonably long experiment. In this case, I could choose to control one of them. If – going back to our example – I want to control prosody, I choose one and only one prosody for the test items. This simplifies the experiment substantially, making it easier and quicker to set-up, even though it may mean running a second experiment with the alternative prosodic structure in the future. Note that balance and control are important for all quantitative work, not only that which might be considered experimental.

In experimental work, a **cell** is a group with shared characteristics. When designing a sociolinguistic experiment, the researcher needs to consider cells that have to do with people (traits of voices, speakers, and listeners) as well as cells that have to do with the structure of language (especially any linguistic factors that are known to be linked with the dependent variable in some way).

When balancing cells, it's helpful to create a table, like the one for the broad social categories shown in Table 1.2. For this experiment (designed to test whether the age and sex attributed to a speaker influence how reliable listeners believe the speakers to be), the age and sex of the voices are balanced. Creating such a table early in the experiment design process provides the researcher with a goal to aim for when creating stimuli and setting up the experiment. But, as we shall see, there are still many steps to take before the experiment can be run, and some of these steps might reveal that the initial goal is unfeasible or even impossible. At each such step, the experimenter must return to the table to check and potentially adjust the numbers, or else rethink the experiment design altogether.

What's that?

Experimental control is when a known variable is constrained so that it does not vary but is, instead, held constant.

Balancing is when we have equal numbers of tokens for each of the possible influencing factors.

Cells are categories of potential influencing factors based on where they intersect.

Stimuli are materials that are expected to cause a response in the participants' behavior.

Talkers are the people perceived to have produced the auditory stimuli in a perception experiment. They are differentiated from **speakers**, who are people who produce speech and who, in experimental work, are most often participants.

People who take part in experiments are variously referred to as **participants** or **subjects**.

A **confederate** is a person who is a part of the experiment (e.g., their behavior changes across conditions) but is not the experimenter or a participant.

Table 1.2 Example of a table used for balancing cells

	Younger	Middle	Older
Females	20	20	20
Males	20	20	20

How do I decide between balancing and controlling a variable? If your hypothesis involves testing an effect of a particular variable, then that variable must be balanced. You might also need to balance a variable in cases when it isn't possible to control it. While it's possible (and common) to balance multiple variables in a single experiment, I recommend that people who are new to experiments strive to control as many variables as possible. This will allow for a simpler experiment, and – when it comes to experimental design – it is a very good idea to keep it simple.

But people can't be put into tidy categories! This feels wrong! One weakness of the experimental method is that it doesn't leave much room for treating every single variable as gradient or overlapping. It's important to remember that all methods have their weaknesses in addition to their strengths, and no method can address all questions on its own. In my opinion, we'll advance the understanding of the relationship between language and society the most by utilizing the vast array of methods at our fingertips, examining the Big Questions from a variety of very different angles. That usually means that we need to compromise on some things that aren't the primary focus of that part of the study.

Remember: as the researcher, you have the power to determine what social characteristics you will use. For example, locally relevant social characteristics or interactive stances and styles might be more relevant for your particular hypothesis. Because relatively few sociolinguists have conducted experimental work, many research questions along these lines remain understudied from an experimental perspective. It is my hope that as a greater number of sociolinguists conduct experimental work, we'll develop more and better ways to explore the more nuanced aspects of language and society, experimentally. Thus, if you are among the group of researchers who wish to use experiments while refraining from using discrete social categories, you can help develop the best ways to do this.

1.2. Experimental methods: who needs them and how do you choose one?

Experimental methods are not for everyone, and they aren't necessary to answer every research question that's worth asking. So how do you know if you need them? The flowchart in Figure 1.1 can begin to answer this question for you. Essentially, it all depends on your research question and goals. Experiments are less natural than other forms of data collection; even those that collect spontaneous speech from interactions between friends are not entirely natural because the researcher has intentionally introduced some factor that they anticipate will affect the speakers' behaviors in some way. I don't see this as a problem because, again, it is my view that experiments provide a range of tools for sociolinguistic work and that they are most powerful for answering sociolinguistic questions when conducted alongside (or having been well-informed by) research using other methods. After all, as stated by the Cumulative Paradox, "the more that is known about a language, the more we can find out about it" (Labov 1972: 202). I suggest that this extends beyond knowledge of

Figure 1.1   A flowchart to help decide whether an experimental method is appropriate

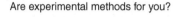

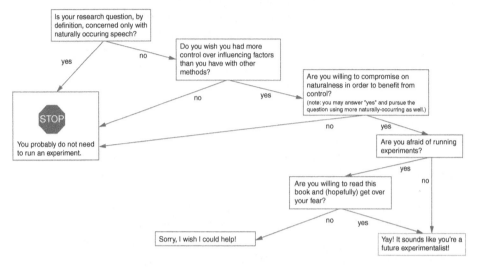

a single language: the more that is known about how language works, in general, the more we can find out about it. And to do that, we need to use multiple methodologies and we need to explore the same Big Questions across diverse communities and language families.

One of the trickiest parts of conducting any type of research is narrowing your research question to something that is both manageable given your level of expertise and realistic given the time frame. The quote from Barbara Johnstone at the beginning of this chapter was in reference to conducting qualitative work, but it also applies to quantitative experimental work: we need to transform our initial hunches into answerable questions, ones that are narrow enough to address within a single study. For experimental work, narrowing the research question has to happen right at the beginning of the research process, before collecting data and even before beginning to design the experiment. Narrowing the research question will allow you to identify the appropriate experimental paradigm and stimuli. In the next section I discuss different classes of research questions, each of which is associated with their own set of experimental paradigms. To help narrow your research question, try to identify the class of questions it falls into. You may find that your interests span across the question classes. If so, great! That's a natural way of building a research program. But, to begin, keep it simple by selecting one of them as a starting place. (See Chapter 7 for more hints on how to narrow your research question.)

Experiments have been used by sociolinguists for years but, over time, they have gotten more common and more sophisticated in their design. In the next section, I introduce a number of studies, describing the research questions and findings but saving the details of the design until later chapters. The descriptions are organized by research question, first beginning with those that focus on perception of speech and/or social characteristics (Section 1.3). Then, we'll move on to those that focus on speech production (Section 1.4). Section 1.5 focuses on studies that examine the production-perception interface, and Section 1.6 discusses those that investigate differences across individuals.

1.3. Perception experiments

First, I step through work that investigates what social cues are attributed to voices or specific linguistic cues in the signal (i.e., how does language use influence person perception?). I then move on to work that explores factors influencing intelligibility (i.e., are all ways of speaking understood with equal ease and accuracy by all listeners?). Finally, I discuss work that uses priming to explore questions of how words, sounds, and other linguistic information is stored in the mind and accessed during speech perception (i.e., do socially associated primes affect how speech is perceived and interpreted?). Included in this last section is research that explores how stereotypes and expectations can influence how an individual perceives speech.

1.3.1. Perceiving speaker characteristics and measuring attitudes

Sociolinguistic experiments have long been used to explore questions about language attitudes. For example, there is a great deal of work investigating what social cues listeners extract from an auditory signal. Some of this work falls under perceptual dialectology, other studies fall within social psychology, and others are geared more toward questions of interest to phoneticians.

Work along these lines draws on the common belief that what language, dialect, or linguistic variant someone uses tells us something about the speaker. Sometimes, the beliefs that are uncovered can help explain some of the sociolinguistic variation we observe in production. For example, if we are looking at language variation across a national border, it would be helpful to know something about the stereotypes and attitudes people in that area have about the other country, the people who live there, and the variables most closely associated with the way they talk.

What people say about other people based only on hearing them speak also reveals stereotypes about the people who are associated with those ways of talking. So if, for example, you are interested in stereotypes about a particular demographic but it isn't politically correct to talk about those stereotypes, you can often still learn about the stereotypes through looking at language stereotypes. Knowing something about these language-based stereotypes – including what they are, when and how they form, and in what ways they affect the lives of speakers – can help sociolinguists combat them.

To explore person perception, rating tasks (Section 3.1.1) are often used. These tasks elicit responses to questions that explicitly ask about a talker's social characteristics. Most commonly, participants listen to a short clip of a talker and they are asked to rate the talker in terms of some social characteristic (e.g., how friendly do you think this person sounds?). By comparing responses to different clips, the researcher can make claims about how linguistic differences between the clips induce perceptions of the different social characteristics and traits.

Work along these lines has sought to identify what social meanings or characteristics are associated with particular languages (Lambert, Hodgson, Gardner, & Fillenbaum 1960; Hilton & Gooskens 2013), styles (Hardeman Guthrie 2016), linguistic variables (Campbell-Kibler 2007; Levon 2007; Szakay 2012), or ways of talking associated with certain broad social characteristics (Purnell, Idsardi, & Baugh 1999). The work has focused on the attribution of a wide range of social characteristics, including ethnicity (Buck 1968; Tucker & Lambert 1969; Bailey & Maynor 1989; Purnell et al. 1999; Thomas & Reaser 2004; Szakay 2008), gender and sexuality (Munson, McDonald, Deboe, & White 2006; Levon 2007; Munson & Babel 2007, Foulkes, Docherty, Khattab, & Yaeger-Dror 2010; Mack & Munson 2012; Zimman 2013; Barron-Lutzross 2016), regional dialect (Bush 1967, Preston 1999, Williams, Garrett, & Coupland 1999), degree of accentedness (Brennan & Brennan 1981), personality traits (Addington 1968; Lambert et al. 1960; Preston 1999; Bayard 2000; Hasty 2015), politeness (Idemaru, Winter, & Brown 2015), credibility (Lev-Ari & Keysar 2010), and occupations (Labov 1972). The answers to these questions can shed light on language attitudes, language-based discrimination (Purnell et al. 1999), and the ways in which the overall impression of a person influences what characteristics are attributed to them, known as halo effects (as described by Ball & Giles 1982 and as observed by Thakerar & Giles 1981). They can also be used to explore questions related to perceived dialect boundaries (Plichta & Preston 2005), how well participants can identify dialects (Preston 1996; Williams et al. 1999; Yonezawa Morris 1999; Flanigan & Norris 2000; Kerswill 2001), or whether language learners acquire socioindexical meanings (Hardeman Guthrie 2016). They can be combined with investigations of the variable in production (e.g., Bailey & Maynor 1989) and there is evidence that responses depend on the participants' prior exposure to people who talk that way (e.g., Clopper &Pisoni 2004).

One of the areas of study that examines person perception is Folk Linguistics, sometimes referred to as Perceptual Dialectology. Map tasks are commonly used in perceptual dialectology. During these tasks, researchers ask participants to mark boundaries and provide labels of dialect boundaries on a blank map. While not inherently experimental, they use the experimental method when the researcher sets out to compare responses across different groups of individuals or if different information is provided on different maps (e.g., different labels or geographic markers) in order to determine how that information might influence responses. In addition to map tasks, Preston (1996) describes multiple methods as part of the perceptual dialectology toolkit, some of which are experimental and are closely tied with other work (discussed above) that looks at the perception of talker characteristics.

Work looking at what social characteristics are attributed to a talker has increasingly focused on the extent to which the social meanings ascribed to a single linguistic variable depend on the rest of the linguistic cues that are present (Campbell-Kibler 2007, 2011; Levon 2007, 2014; Pharao, Maegaard, Spindler Møller, & Kristiansen 2014; Walker, García, Cortés, & Campbell-Kibler 2014). Relatedly, social information attributed to a talker can influence the social meanings of variants produced by that talker (see e.g., Thakerar & Giles 1981; Campbell-Kibler 2010a). This work explores how clusters of linguistic variables, together, contribute to the perception of a talker's style, and it demonstrates that a single variable is interpreted within the context of what other variants are present in the signal and what social characteristics are attributed to the talker.

Other work along these lines explores the nature of the sociolinguistic monitor (Labov, Ash, Ravindranath, Weldon, & Nagy 2011; Wagner & Hesson 2014; Levon & Buchstaller 2015). The monitor is said to track the frequency of sociolinguistic variants, attributing characteristics to the speaker based on a combination of the frequency of the variants in the signal and the stored social meanings of the variants. The question of how participants respond to the frequency of variants (as opposed to simply the presence of a variant) is an interesting one that warrants further exploration with a wider range of linguistic variables and the employment of a variety of different experimental paradigms. Designs that lessen the salience of both the social information and the linguistic variants could yield especially enlightening insights.

In addition, there is a small amount of exciting work exploring when children acquire knowledge of sociolinguistic associations. The ability to differentiate different dialects begins early; five- and seven-month-old infants can differentiate their native dialect from non-native dialects (Butler, Floccia, Goslin, & Panneton 2011). Likewise, young children from at least some regions demonstrate a preference for their native dialect (Kinzler & DeJesus 2013) but do not yet classify dialects based on stereotypes (Kinzler & DeJesus 2013) and are not yet able to categorize their native dialect as separate from a non-native dialect (Wagner, Clopper, & Pate 2014). By the age of nine, children categorize dialects in line with general language-based stereotypes (Kinzler & DeJesus 2013).

Explore the methods

Materials from the following studies that investigate the social meaning associated with language can be found on the companion website: https://www.bloomsbury.com/cw/experimental-research-methods-in-sociolinguistics/

ethnicity

Purnell et al. (1999)

professionalism

Levon and Buchstaller (2015)

multiple traits

Campbell-Kibler (2007, 2011)

Levon (2007, 2014)

While some scholars have argued that responses on rating tasks reflect participants' subconscious attitudes (Kristiansen 2009), others have argued that such tasks are successful at acquiring only so-called explicit associations or explicit attitudes: those stereotypes and attitudes that participants don't mind owning up to. While there is much less sociolinguistic work exploring questions about implicit associations than explicit ones, there are clear benefits to being able to elicit attitude data in ways that do not allow participants to skew results with dishonest or misleading responses. Thus, we now turn to a discussion of methods that were designed with the intention of eliciting implicit associations or implicit attitudes: those that participants might suppress but that are present nonetheless.

The Implicit Association Test (IAT) is the most widely used task to explore implicit associations. The IAT aims to reveal associations that the participant may not know they have or may not want to admit to having (see Section 3.1.4 for a description of the method). The IAT was developed in social psychology by Greenwald, McGhee, and Schwartz (1998) and has since been adopted into sociolinguistics (Babel 2009, 2010; Campbell-Kibler 2012; Pantos & Perkins 2012). Babel (2009) is an excellent example of effective use of the IAT.

While both implicit and explicit measures correlate with behavior, there is evidence that there is less variability in the size of the effect with implicit measures (Greenwald, Poelman, Uhlmann, & Banaji 2009). However, it is unclear the extent to which the IAT is effective at measuring what it aims to measure. First, while a comparison of reaction times to categorization in the different blocks likely includes a component related to the strength of the association between the target concept and the attribute/valence, this is not the only factor contributing to the recorded reaction time. Different participants – and the same participant at different points in the experiment – may be better at suppressing stereotypes than others. This means that the IAT may be a better measure of the ability to suppress stereotypes than it is a measure of implicit associations. Second, the hypothesis is not disguised in these types of tasks, adding weight to the concern that the task measures stereotype suppression; if people are aware of the hypothesis, there are more top-down processes influencing behavior and, as a result, it's difficult to say what exactly the data show. Third, if there is a correlation between implicit measures and explicit measures (which some scholars have argued is proof that the task works or have used the correlation to determine the appropriate treatment of the data post-collection (Greenwald, Nosek, & Banaji 2003)), then it suggests that Kristiansen (2009) is correct in his claim that rating tasks elicit subconscious attitudes, and it's not clear why a simpler task eliciting so-called explicit measures can't be used instead. Fourth, some of the methods that have become standard for analyzing IAT data are not standard for analyzing reaction times more generally, which raises questions as to whether they really are the best methods for analysis. (These are discussed following the presentation of how to design an IAT in Section 3.1.4.) So while the IAT is intended to address valid concerns with other methods, much more work is needed to determine when results from an IAT are meaningful and valid.

An alternative to the IAT is an auditory affective priming experiment, where valenced primes are meant to result in faster responses for similarly valenced targets. While the method is not commonly used within sociolinguistics, Speelman, Spruyt, Impe, and Geeraerts (2013) use it to examine attitudes toward different dialects of Dutch. However, the extent to which the task is really about language attitudes is unclear, and further work is needed to adapt the methodology for sociolinguistic questions.

Another alternative to IAT is the Social Category Association Test (SCAT), developed by Llamas, Watt, and MacFarlane (2016). The difference between the IAT and SCAT is that, unlike the IAT, there are no incorrect responses with SCAT; the strength of an association is determined by a combination of the response and the time it took to make the response. In addition, rather than testing the association between the two categories given on the screen, it tests the strength of an association between a stimulus (e.g., an auditory stimulus of the word *red*, with /r/ pronounced [ɾ]) and a label (e.g., Scotland vs. not Scotland). The SCAT has some of the same limitations as the IAT; for example, comparing behavior across participants is problematic because the variation may be due to factors other than the participants' implicit associations. However, for the purpose used by Llamas et al. (2016) (i.e., identifying which variables have sociolinguistic salience), it seems appropriate. Also, it has the added benefit of not reinforcing an arbitrary association during the training sessions and, when appropriate fillers are used, it is less likely to induce overt suppression of implicit associations among the participants.

A description of how to conduct an IAT is presented in Section 3.1.4, alongside explanations of related-methodologies, such as SCAT.

Explore the methods

Materials from the following studies that explore implicit associations between social factors and language can be found on the companion website: https://www.bloomsbury.com/cw/experimental-research-methods-in-sociolinguistics/

Implicit Association Test (IAT)

Babel (2009)

Social Category Association Test (SCAT)

Llamas et al. (2016)

1.3.2. The processing and intelligibility of native and non-native dialects and forms

Many of us, at one time or another, have had trouble understanding someone who speaks a different dialect than we do. Normally, however, we are able to adapt quickly (Clarke & Garrett 2004), but the extent to which adaptation occurs depends at least partially on contextually relevant information (Kraljic & Samuel 2011). Work investigating the intelligibility of non-native dialects and forms – as well as work examining processing costs associated with listening to such forms – identifies a number of factors that contribute to how well one understands a dialect that they do not speak. In addition, such work sheds light on the nature of what kinds of phonetic information must be linked to the phonological level, and suggests that – while phonetic distance seems to have the largest effect (Gooskens, Heeringa, & Beijering 2008) – morphosyntactic variation also affects intelligibility (Hilton, Gooskens, & Shüppert 2013).

The belief that socioindexical variation is a critical component of language is widely held among sociolinguists. However, in many traditional models of word recognition, interspeaker variability is unaccounted for, and it is assumed that variability is irrelevant for processing abstract information, such as lexical information. Work on interspeaker and interdialect intelligibility challenges this view, demonstrating how word recognition and comprehension are influenced by the talker's age (Jacewicz & Fox 2012) and regional dialect (Labov, Yaeger, & Steiner 1972; Ash 1988 as described by Labov 2010: chapter 3; Floccia, Goslin, Girard, & Konopcznski 2006; Jacewicz & Fox 2012). Relatedly, the talker's dialect also influences speed of accessing more abstract semantic information, such as animacy (Adank & McQueen 2007), and a lag in processing speed that results from lower intelligibility appears to affect the talker's perceived credibility (Lev-Ari & Keysar 2010).

There is a great deal of work exploring the role of the listener's past experience on the processing and intelligibility of non-native dialects and forms (Floccia et al. 2006; Labov 2010; Dufour, Brunellière, & Nguyen 2013). In their work on the perception of New York English, Sumner and Samuel (2009) found that speed of lexical access was influenced by the participants' (and their families') history in the region. Likewise, in a cross-modal priming study on the perception of two dialects of Catalan, Llompart and Simonet (forthcoming) found that listeners who spoke the standard variety received less priming after exposure to a regional (non-standard) variety whereas listeners who spoke the non-standard variety were equally primed by both dialects. Signers, too, are influenced by such factors; for example, participants are more accurate at identifying color terms for dialects they natively sign, and the identification of signs from dialects other than their own is higher for participants with Deaf parents (Stamp 2016). However, the role of exposure is not straightforward, as in-group status does not necessarily aid word identification (Labov & Ash 1997; Labov 2010) and effects of exposure can vary across different linguistic variables (Clopper, Pierrehumbert, & Tamati 2010; Labov 2010). In a word recognition task with noise, Clopper and Tamati (2010) observed a same-dialect benefit only in the second block, in which some words from the first block were repeated (described in more detail in Clopper 2014). While many scholars have proposed that language attitudes and intelligibility are linked (see e.g., Wolff 1959), the exact role that attitudes play remains elusive (Schüppert, Hilton, & Gooskens 2015).

There is also evidence that intelligibility can be influenced by social information extracted from visual stimuli. Rubin (1992) demonstrates that students rate a non-native English-speaking instructor as less intelligible and as having a stronger accent when the instructor is shown as Chinese rather than Caucasian. Likewise, Babel and Russell (2015) observed a decrease in intelligibility for listeners shown a Chinese Canadian face though ratings of accentedness did not shift, and McGowan (2015) demonstrates that transcription accuracy is influenced by a combination of the listener's stereotypes and the ethnicity of the person in the photograph. Thus, listeners' expectations about how their interlocutor will talk can influence how well they understand their interlocutor's speech. Efforts to reduce the effect have not always been successful (Rubin 1992), but through gaining a better understanding of how, when, and why such effects occur, we will be better equipped to develop effective tools to combat stereotypes and the negative effects they have on people's lives.

A number of different methods can be used to explore questions about the processing and intelligibility of non-native dialects, including lexical decision and semantic decision tasks (Section 3.2.11), word recognition tasks (Section 3.2.2), transcription tasks (Section 3.2.7), gating tasks (Section 3.2.10), and experiments that involve priming (Section 2.1.7).

Explore the methods

Select materials from the following studies can be found on the companion website: https://www.bloomsbury.com/cw/experimental-research-methods-in-sociolinguistics/

intelligibility

Hilton et al. (2013)

social priming influencing intelligibility

McGowan (2015)

past experience influencing intelligibility

Llompart and Simonet (forthcoming)

1.3.3. Social information priming linguistic behavior

There is a growing body of work that examines the ways in which language production and perception can be primed by social information. This line

of work largely relies on methods adapted from those used in psycholinguistics and experimental phonetics and phonology. Many of these studies
are conducted with the aim of integrating social information into cognitive
models of production and perception though they can also be used to shed
light on, for example, the role of attention in sociolinguistic processing.
Such shifts in perception also have real-life consequences and could potentially be linked with some of the intelligibility results described in Section
1.3.2 and the work on person perception discussed in Section 1.3.1.

Early work in this vein focuses on the speech of bilinguals, examining the ways in which bilinguals' perception of sounds shift depending
on what language they believe they are listening to, with the strongest
bilinguals being affected the most (Elman, Diehl, & Buchwald 1977).
In addition, there is work demonstrating that how listeners perceive
sounds is influenced by phonetic realizations they encountered earlier
in the sentence (Ladefoged & Broadbent 1957). Later work extends this
research further into the social realm, identifying how social characteristics attributed to a voice appear to influence how sounds are perceived (Strand & Johnson 1996; Drager 2005; Munson, Jefferson, &
McDonald 2006; Babel & McGuire 2013). In order to determine that
shifts in phone perception result from so-called top down social information (rather than a characteristic of the voice that is both correlated
with perceived social characteristics and influences sound perception),
visual primes (i.e., photographs and video) have also been used. This
work demonstrates that shifts in phone perception are related to the
listener's perception of the talker's gender (Strand & Johnson 1996;
Johnson, Strand, & D'Imperio 1999; Strand 1999; Munson 2011),
regional origin (Niedzielski 1999; Hay, Nolan, & Drager 2006), ethnicity (Staum Casasanto 2008), social class (Hay, Warren, & Drager
2006), age (Hay et al. 2006b; Koops, Gentry, & Pantos 2008; Drager
2011), and attractiveness (McGuire & Babel 2015), at least when the
sounds are temporarily ambiguous (Koops 2011). Items linked with
social characteristics – such as stuffed toys associated with different
regions (Hay & Drager 2010) – also appear to have some influence on
the perception of sounds for at least some listeners, providing evidence
that the effects of social information on the perception of sounds is,
to some degree, automatic in terms of the underlying cognitive mechanisms that are at play. Further evidence that such shifts stem from automatic processes rather than overt expectations about the speaker comes
from work demonstrating that perception can also be influenced by dialects of other speakers the listener is exposed to prior to completing the
task (Hay, Drager, & Warren 2010). There is even evidence that socioindexical information inherent in the signal can speed lexical access across
bilinguals' languages (Szakay, Babel, & King 2016).

Similarly, accessing social information seems to slow when lexical information is stereotypically at odds with characteristics attributed to the talker; when classifying different talkers as male or female, listeners are slower to respond if the target lexical item is a word (e.g., *man*) that refers to someone of the opposite sex (Green & Barber 1981: Exp 1 & 2), is an opposite-sex name (Green & Barber 1981: Exp 4), or is a word that is stereotypically associated with the opposite sex (Most, Sorber, & Cunningham 2007). Further, the processing of grammatical gender in languages like Spanish also seems to be influenced by the talker's perceived gender (Vitevitch, Sereno, Jongman, & Goldstein 2013). Age has also been tested, with work providing evidence that words are accessed more quickly in a lexical decision task when the talker age they are stereotypically associated with is congruent with the age attributed to the voice (Kim 2016). Interestingly, such effects exist even when the words are not stereotypically associated with talkers of different ages but tend to be used more by speakers of certain ages nevertheless (Walker & Hay 2011).

In addition to the work on sound perception, there is a limited amount of work investigating the extent to which social information influences grammaticality judgments of syntactic and morphosyntactic variation (Walker 2008; Squires 2013a). Much more work along these lines is needed to determine the extent to which social information influences processing of (morpho-)syntactic information, and the extent to which interactions between social factors and phonetic detail affect the perception and anticipation of syntactic structures. With a little creativity, brave researchers who wish to advance the field in this direction could have a substantial impact, demonstrating the importance of integrating the social side of language into our models of sentence processing.

In addition to the body of work that demonstrates an effect of social primes on the perception of linguistic variables, there is evidence that such effects are inconsistently observed (Squires 2013ab; Chang 2015; Lawrence 2015; Walker 2016). Further, many of the studies that observe an effect provide evidence that the effect is found with only some subsets of the population (Hay & Drager 2010; Drager 2011). Replication of the findings using a wide range of settings, languages, linguistic variables, and methods is needed to fully understand when, why, and how social information influences the perception of linguistic variables.

The evidence that social factors can influence speech perception and processing – even if only some of the time – has important methodological implications. If exposure to different individuals or to the concept of different regions can affect perception, then we would expect that participants who interact with different experimenters might demonstrate different behavior on experimental tasks. Indeed, such effects have been shown for the production and perception of segments (Hay et al. 2006ab, 2009) as well as the perception of tones (Brunelle & Jannedy 2013), and they have been observed in a range of different kinds of tasks (Hay et al. 2010). Because the effect has been observed even when it was unintentional (Hay et al. 2006ab)[1], this should serve as a grave warning for projects where data collection is conducted by more than one experimenter: the experimenter and location should be controlled. If more than one experimenter must be used (e.g., the student researcher who is in charge of collecting data graduates but more data collection is needed), experimenter identity should be tested as an independent variable in the analysis, both in isolation and in interaction with relevant factors (e.g., dialect of the stimuli). In addition, different participants may not behave the same way with a single experimenter (Stanford 2010), so it's also important to collect demographic information from participants and to consider possible differences in participant behavior that could be due to social factors (e.g., the power structure in the community).

An understudied area within sociolinguistics but one with sociolinguistic implications nonetheless (see e.g., variationist studies on affect and attitudes) is work that focuses on the effect of emotions on speech production and perception. Work on the role of emotion would benefit from a more nuanced understanding of social factors, perhaps resulting in a more nuanced understanding of emotion. Furthermore, sociolinguists could explore the role emotions play in accommodation and how it might influence language attitudes and the effects of language attitudes on speech production and perception.

Explore the methods

Materials from the following studies that investigate the effect of social priming on perception can be found on the companion website: https://www.bloomsbury.com/cw/experimental-research-methods-in-sociolinguistics/

sounds

Babel & McGuire (2013)

Niedzielski (1999)

the lexicon

Kim (2016)

Walker and Hay (2011)

syntax

Squires (2013a)

---

[1] Oops! Sometimes I guess I have to learn the hard way.

1.4. Production experiments

There is a large body of work demonstrating that speakers shift the way they talk depending on their social goals and who they are talking to (Giles 1973; Giles & Powesland 1975; Natale 1975; Bell 1984; Pardo 2006), converging on or diverging from the speech of their interlocutor. Speakers' realizations are also influenced by characteristics associated with people referred to in the discourse (Mendoza-Denton et al. 2003) and the topic being discussed (Love & Walker 2012), and recent work demonstrates that accommodation is not limited to spoken languages but is also found in signed languages (Stamp, Schembri, Evans, & Cormier 2016). Some of the work along these lines has analyzed spontaneously produced speech. For example, Mendoza-Denton et al. (1999) analyzed Oprah's speech, comparing her productions across different referees. Likewise, Llamas, Watt, and Johnson (2009) conducted a study where individual participants met with different interviewers. However, spontaneously produced speech is not always desirable, either because it does not provide a balanced number of items across the different target variables (some variables can be too infrequent to study using spontaneous speech data) or because it does not offer the level of control needed for the specific research question. Thus, some scholars have relied on speech elicited using alternative, lab-based methods (e.g., Pardo 2006; Babel 2012). In these studies, speakers produce the same lexical items across conditions, controlling not only the phonological environment but also the word. To achieve this, the researchers use map tasks (Section 4.4.1) and imitation studies (Section 4.4.4).

Two of the research questions that are currently being explored in the sociolinguistic literature on accommodation are: with what variables do we observe accommodation, and what is it about the different variables that influences whether accommodation is observed? Speakers do not shift equally across all linguistic variables; when it comes to sounds, more acoustic distance between the participant and the voice/interlocutor leaves more room for convergence to occur (Babel 2012; Walker & Campbell-Kibler 2015). But accommodation is also observed at other levels of the grammar. Speakers converge on morphological and morphosyntactic forms (Szmrecsanyi 2005; Beckner, Rácz, Hay, Brandstetter, & Bartneck 2016) produced by an interlocutor, but identifying which ones and understanding why those ones shift in particular still requires more work. Which variables exhibit a shift can interact in interesting ways with the dialect of the talker (i.e., voice) and speaker (i.e., participant) (Walker & Campbell-Kibler 2015), social characteristics of the participant (Babel 2012), and characteristics such as attractiveness attributed to the talker (Babel 2012). While convergence is generally not observed between first and second language speakers (Kim, Horton, & Bradlow 2011), it is found for native speakers of different dialects, especially for variables that are most distinct (Walker & Campbell-Kibler 2015).

Another question is concerned with the role of speaker attitudes: to what extent do the attitudes of the speaker toward their interlocutor or the language variety influence the degree and direction of accommodation? It seems that attitudes toward other varieties (and toward the people who speak those varieties) influence the direction and degree of accommodation (Llamas et al. 2009).

Some of this also work explores the extent to which agency is required to observe accommodation. That accommodation occurs even when participants complete a non-social task listening to a recording (e.g., Babel 2012) suggests that the process is, to some degree, automatic. This position is strengthened by work by Walker and Campbell-Kibler (2015), who observed convergence despite explicitly instructing the participants to produce the words "in their own voice" (Walker & Campbell-Kibler 2015: 5). Further, there is evidence that accommodation also occurs in virtual reality contexts, even though the virtual interlocutor cannot interpret the linguistic behavior (Staum Casasanto, Jasmin, & Casasanto 2010). However, there appear to be limits, as accommodation does not appear to occur when interacting with a robot (Beckner et al. 2016). Thus, it seems highly likely that speaker agency can still play a role, but what that role might be and when it might come into play remains an open question. Certainly, social factors play a key role (Pardo 2012) and some scholars have suggested cognitive mechanisms through which this occurs (Drager, Hay, & Walker 2010; Babel 2012; Pardo 2012). Much more work using of a wider range of methods is necessary to fully answer these questions.

Explore the methods

Materials from the following studies can be found on the companion website: https://www.bloomsbury.com/cw/experimental-research-methods-in-sociolinguistics/

imitation tasks

Walker and Campbell-Kibler (2015)

1.5. A link between production and perception

There is a large body of work that examines the link between an individual's production and their perception. Within phonology, there is work on first language acquisition (e.g., Edwards 1974), second language acquisition (e.g., Sheldon & Strange 1982), and bilingualism (e.g., Beach, Burnham, & Kitamura 2001). This work is important because it can shed light on the nature of mental representations of phonological information and the cognitive mechanisms that are at play. Further, it can help shed light on how sound change occurs. For example, work on the production and perception of mergers and near-mergers indicates that phoneme distinctions persist in production even when listeners cannot distinguish the sounds during perception (Labov, Yaeger, & Steiner 1972, Ch. 6; Costa & Mattingly 1981; Janson & Schulman 1983; Labov, Karen, & Miller 1991). However, in some cases, listeners are able to differentiate between sounds undergoing merger even when they do not produce the distinction themselves (Hay et al. 2006b). Likewise, the link between the production and perception of regional variation is not straightforward (Fridland & Kendall 2012), and while shifts over time may occur in production, there is not always a corresponding shift in perception (Evans & Iverson 2007).

There are still many questions that remain. For example, does social information affect the link between production and perception beyond correlations between social factors and the linguistic phenomenon being tested (e.g., merger or language acquisition)? In addition, while most of this work focuses on sounds, there are a number of interesting questions to ask for other levels of the grammar, and for interactions between sounds and other levels of the grammar. For instance, one could explore whether the degree to which exposure to a prime biases a listener's interpretation of a non-standard construction is linked with how likely that participant is to produce the construction.

One challenge of this line of inquiry is that it most often requires expertise with experimental methods in both production and perception, potentially increasing time to data collection. On the plus side, this means gaining experience with a wider range of methods. Alternatively, a perception experiment can be tacked on to a production study that uses sociolinguistic methods that are already familiar to the researcher.

1.6. Individual differences

Researchers have long known that there is individual variation in behavior during experimental tasks. This variation is often treated as a problem that should be overcome with statistical techniques (through the use of, e.g., mixed effects models). However, the presence of variation can indicate that there is an unidentified factor influencing behavior. In addition to attitudinal, exposure-based, and other social and linguistic factors, scholars have begun to identify factors that appear to be related to some of the previously undescribed variation, factors which have interesting implications for sociolinguistic work.

One such factor is personality type, which, in past work, has been identified and measured using the Broad Autism Phenotype Questionnaire (BAPQ) (Hurley, Losh, Parlier, Reznick, & Piven 2007), the Empathy Quotient, or the Autism Spectrum Quotient (AQ) (Baron-Cohen & Wheelwright 2004; Wheelwright et al. 2006). When completing the tasks, participants provide self-rated responses to questions that are designed to measure the degree to which they fall into three trait categories: Aloof (e.g., "I enjoy being in social situations," where a low agreement rating results in a higher score for aloofness), Pragmatic Language ("I have been told that I talk too much about certain topics"), and Rigid ("I am comfortable with unexpected changes in plans"). There is some evidence that responses on the BAPQ (or to the question subsets) correlate with behavior on some linguistic tasks, influencing, for example, the degree to which speakers converge on phonetic realizations they're exposed to (Yu, Abrego-Collier, & Sonderegger 2013) and the extent to which listeners are influenced by contextual information during sound categorization (Yu 2010). There is also evidence that such measures can predict the extent to which a listener's attribution of professionalism to a talker will be influenced by the rate of occurrence of sociolinguistic variants in that talker's speech (Levon & Buchstaller 2015).

Thus, there is a great deal of work that would benefit from a closer look at the role of different personality types, determining when and to what extent these factors play a role. For those of you embarking on this path, however, I offer a word of caution: except in cases when, prior to data collection, the hypothesis is clearly laid out and the plan for testing the relationship between the linguistic behavior and the results from the questionnaire

Explore the methods

Materials from the following studies that examine the effects of individual/personality traits on linguistic behavior can be found on the companion website: https://www.bloomsbury.com/cw/experimental-research-methods-in-sociolinguistics/

Levon and Buchstaller (2015)

Yu (2010)

A copy of the BAPQ, along with instructions for the participant and researcher, is provided in Appendix A in Hurley et al. (2007).

are set, the risk of false positives is high. Replication is, therefore, essential. It is also important to consider whether all questions are appropriate for the speech community being studied. In addition, the use of tasks that do not require the participant to self-report may prove fruitful.

1.7. Chapter summary

In this chapter, I have provided an overview of sociolinguistic work conducted using experimental techniques. The chapter is intended to:

- provide you with an overview of the types of sociolinguistic research questions that have been addressed using experimental methods, and

- suggest some interesting avenues for future research within each of the topics of interest.

One glaring omission from this chapter is a section describing the many different ways that corpus-based, variationist methods have contributed to sociolinguistic theory. One reason for this is that this book is intended to promote experimental methods that offer more control as well as to improve the methodology being used in sociolinguistic experiments. In addition, there are a number of excellent resources that already exist for variationist work, some of which are broad in scope (e.g., Bayley & Lucas 2007) and some of which are narrower, focusing on a specific set of questions or variables (e.g., Ravindranath 2015; Pichler 2016). There are many different theoretical angles to such work, and describing them all would require much more space than I have here. Thus, readers who are interested but unfamiliar with such methods are enthusiastically encouraged to check out these alternative sources.

As discussed in the chapter, there is a long history of experimental methods in sociolinguistics, but there remain a number of questions that have yet to be fully addressed. In Chapters 3–5, I step through how to set up and conduct various experimental paradigms. Before describing specific paradigms, however, I present guidelines in Chapter 2 that are to be applied to all experimental work.

Main points

- Experiments are a powerful tool but may not be appropriate for everyone.

- Let the research question guide you to a method, not the other way around. Identify which line of research described in this chapter interests you most, and then focus on the methods researchers in that area tend to use.

- To identify your research question: read. If one of the research areas described here sounds interesting, check out the work for yourself and read related work, such as that cited therein.

Further reading

Campbell-Kibler, Kathyrn (2010). Sociolinguistics and perception. *Language and Linguistics Compass* 3(1): 1–13.

Drager, Katie (2010). Sociophonetic variation in speech perception. *Language and Linguistics Compass* 4(7): 473–480.

Hay, Jennifer and Katie Drager (2007). Sociophonetics. *Annual Review of Anthropology* 36: 89–103.

Labov, William (2010). *Principles of Linguistic Change 3: Cognitive and cultural factors*. Oxford, UK: Wiley-Blackwell.

Thomas, Erik (2002). Sociophonetic applications of speech perception experiments. *American Speech* 77(2): 115–147.

Thomas, Erik (2011). *Sociophonetics: An introduction*. Basingstoke: Palgrave Macmillan.

Warren, Paul and Jennifer Hay (2012). Methods and experimental design for studying sociophonetic variation. In Abigail C. Cohn, Cécile Fougeron, and Marie K. Huffman (Eds.) *The Oxford Handbook of Laboratory Phonology*, Oxford University Press, 634–642.

Some practicalities when running experiments

2

Chapter outline

Preparation is the most difficult part.

– Erik Thomas (2002: 130)

And it is also the most important.

– me (here)

2.1. Logistics of running an experiment

There are many things to consider when designing an experiment, and – in order to avoid wasting time and energy – it's important to consider all of them early on. In this chapter, I discuss some aspects of experimental design that are helpful to know about before deciding on the exact design of the experiment. This includes advantages and disadvantages of working with certain data types, as well as some ideas to keep in mind regardless of the experiment design used or the type of data collected.

Know that it's normal to have lots of questions about how to design an experiment and, in some cases, to select imperfect options. One reason it can be difficult is that there is rarely a one-size-fits-all answer; the answer will depend on a combination of your research question and your experience. If you don't have much experience yet with experimental design, I highly recommend choosing the simplest design that will address your research question (or some part of your research question) without compromising control. In a twist of the quote commonly attributed to Albert Einstein: experiments should be made as simple as possible, but not simpler.

2.1.1. Getting the right stimuli: recording and design

People who are new to experimental work are often surprised by how long it takes to set up an experiment, but it's completely normal for the most difficult and time-consuming part of the entire process to be stimulus creation and testing. This is largely because you need to be very careful that your experimental stimuli are both appropriate and controlled. In regard to appropriateness, you want to be sure that – should you get a null result – it's not due to something about how the experiment was set up or about the stimuli you selected. Also, you need to make sure that the stimuli actually test the specific research question you're asking. For example, you may intend to examine the effect of the perceived age of a voice and therefore create stimuli using recordings of people of different ages. However, if listeners don't perceive those voices as belonging to people of different ages, your experiment isn't actually testing your hypothesis.

Control across stimuli is extremely important, and you should control as many factors as possible across your different stimuli. Failing to do so may result in undesirable (and uninteresting) biases in the participants' behavior. There may be some cases where control isn't possible. When factors can't be controlled, they should be balanced. Also, it is imperative that you're aware of the effects that different factors might have on behavior so that you can consider them during analysis, potentially including them as predicting (control) factors in your statistical analysis. For example, lexical frequency is known to be linked with both speed of access during perception and phonetic realizations during production. It should, therefore, be either controlled or balanced across conditions. The content of the utterance, number of syllables (for words), number of words (for utterances), and overall duration of each stimulus should also be considered.

Different kinds of experiments require different kinds of stimuli. Further, some stimuli might work well for one community but not for another. Four major kinds of stimuli in sociolinguistic experiments are: auditory (e.g., audio files of sounds, words, utterances, or even noise), visual (e.g., pictures, silent video, items in the experimental environment, and a non-speaking experimenter or confederate), audio-visual (e.g., video, or a confederate who interacts with the participant), and textual (e.g., written words or sentences). Experiments often contain more than one stimulus type (e.g., auditory and visual). In all cases, care must be taken to maintain as much control over non-test factors as possible across different items within each stimulus type.

A common type of stimuli in sociolinguistic work is **auditory stimuli**. These are used in perception experiments conducted on spoken languages, and they're used in many production experiments, too. The stimuli can be created using natural speech or synthesized speech. If natural, they can be clips from spontaneously produced speech from conversations or they can be highly controlled speech that was produced in a lab. In subfields like psycholinguistics and experimental phonology, most auditory stimuli are either (re)synthesized speech or lab-produced speech, providing the utmost control over a wide range of linguistic factors. However, for the research questions that sociolinguists ask, sometimes more natural-sounding stimuli are more appropriate. It all depends on your research question and the experimental design.

What's that?

Auditory stimuli are those that use only sound. In linguistic work, this is often speech, but it can also include other kinds of noise.

Visual stimuli commonly include photographs, moving images and drawings, but can also include objects.

Audio-visual stimuli are those that incorporate both auditory and visual information.

Textual stimuli are made up of written words.

Regardless of the degree of naturalness of the speech itself, it's important to collect the recordings with as little background noise as possible. Not only does noise make resynthesis nearly impossible, but background noise can affect speakers' behavior on the task. When producing speech in noise, speakers adjust their phonetic realizations (Lombard 1911; Draegert 1951). Some of the shifts could result in realizations that are socially indexed, which could affect subsequent perception of the speech in unintended (and largely unknown) ways. Thus, recordings should be made in the quietest space possible, keeping in mind the naturalness of the speech. Recordings should not be made outside if it can be avoided since wind and background noise can easily render them unusable. Ideally, recordings are made indoors in a sound-attenuated booth or, for more conversational speech, a sound-attenuated room. If using a room, ensure that there are no hard surfaces that bounce sound; tile floors, hard walls and ceilings, and windows can all contribute to unwanted noise (see Cieri 2011). Rugs and curtains can work wonders in making a space recording-friendly. (Or – provided that the people you are recording are as patient as the ones I've worked with – a great recording environment can be achieved using a closet full of clothes!) Wherever you conduct the recording, make sure that there is no computer or other device running and that the recording device is running on batteries (as opposed to being plugged into the wall) to reduce feedback.

Now, assuming you have the appropriate space picked out, there are a few other things to consider when recording sound files to be used as auditory stimuli:

- Use a high quality recorder.
- Record using high settings and a non-lossy format, like wav. You can always downsize the size of the file if you need to, but you can't go back and change an existing file into a higher quality recording after the fact; saving an existing low quality or lossy-format file (e.g., mp3) with higher settings or in a non-lossy format doesn't result in a higher quality recording than what you started off with.
- If the speaker is reading the prompt off of a piece of paper, use a clipboard so the paper doesn't rustle.
- Design the prompt so that you get the intonation you need. This can mean adding extra words to the beginning and ends of lists so you don't end up with list intonation, or it could mean asking them to repeat utterances played from a recording.
- Record a larger number of potential stimuli than you'll actually need, and maybe even some you don't plan to use right away but could potentially use in the future.
- Record each stimuli more than once so you can choose the best one based on, for example, clarity or fluency.
- Make sure the batteries you use are fresh so you don't have to do a battery change mid-recording or, worse, lose a part of the recording because the batteries ran out.

After the initial recording, the recording is normally segmented into smaller files. Each file is given an easily interpretable name that identifies the speaker (usually using a pseudonym) and a unique identifier for the utterance, like the target word or the word at the disambiguation point (e.g., SpeakerPseudonym-IdentifyingWord-TokenNumber.wav, so something like Maria-sharks1.wav and Tony-jets2.wav). Once all tokens for all speakers have been segmented and named in this way, they normally need to be set to the same volume. (I use Praat for this, but other software, such as Audacity, also have this capability.)

Rather than using fully synthesized stimuli (i.e., sounds created from scratch through, e.g., combining sine waves), most sociolinguistic work that does not use natural speech stimuli uses resynthesized speech. Resynthesis is easier to conduct, and natural-sounding stimuli can usually be achieved (though it requires a combination of recordings with no background noise and a whole lot of patience). I normally use Praat to conduct resynthesis and have had the best luck using modified versions of Praat scripts found online or shared among researchers. Links to repositories of resynthesized speech and Praat scripts to conduct resynthesis are provided on the companion website.

A few tips for resynthesis:

- Start with clean recordings. The less background noise, the better.
- When splicing sounds together or modifying only some portion of a signal, boundaries should occur at points where the waveform crosses zero (known as zero crossings).
- Some voices are more difficult to resynthesize than others, especially when it comes to vowel formants. Breathiness and creakiness can both interfere with how successful the resynthesis is.

Like with auditory stimuli, we need to consider a large number of variables when creating **visual stimuli**. Visual stimuli are most commonly images, like a picture of a person or thing, but colors and silent films can also be visual stimuli. Even a poster on the wall or the presence of a non-speaking person who is in the room can serve as visual stimuli.

Different kinds of visual stimuli introduce different considerations. The biggest concern with using colors (or colored images) as visual stimuli is that not all colors attract the same amount of attention. Therefore, when using images, you might want to use black and white images, especially if responses in the experimental paradigm you're using vary depending on attention (e.g., eye-tracking). However, if colors are critical for the study, then be sure to set up your study in a way to avoid any confounds with the attention-grabbing properties of certain colors. This can be attained by balancing across different groups of participants (e.g., purple is associated with A for one group of participants but B for another group), controlling for attention biases by norming ahead of time and only using colors that are similar in terms of the degree to which they attract attention. Alternatively, you could balance items across color groups so that you can be sure any effect you observe is not due to the differences in the colors themselves (as done in a Stroop-like experiment, Stroop 1935).

Beyond color, there are a number of additional things to consider when using images. These are especially important if you are investigating reaction times or eye movements but, even if you are using a different paradigm, it's a good idea to consider whether they could potentially influence behavior on the task. Size and shape matter: participants' attention will be drawn to items that are either larger or much smaller than the items around it. Likewise, differences in orientation and shape can attract attention. Thus, you should avoid differences when possible or, if control is not possible, balance them across conditions appropriately. The style of the images should be matched as closely as possible across all of the images used. Photographs usually introduce more variation in the image than drawings, and control is especially difficult if the photographs involve people. Care must be taken to properly norm photographs so that unintended factors don't influence participant behavior. If using drawings, all images should be drawings and, ideally, should come from the same artist.

Now, where to get images to be used as stimuli? Assuming that you have the appropriate permissions, using a preexisting image can be a great way to cut down on time spent on stimulus creation. There are a number of websites with freely available images that have already been lovingly rated and standardized by psychologists and psycholinguists (see e.g., http://www.cogsci.nl/stimulus-sets#psychological-image-collection-at-stirling-pics). If you're unable to find what you need from a pre-rated image archive, Creative Commons (https://creativecommons.org) is also a great resource. Sometimes, however, the images that we need are so specific that there is little chance of finding them on a preexisting archive. For example, I might be interested in the way that speakers from different dialect areas differ in their use of auxiliary verbs across different verb classes or different subject types. Unless I'm adding the dialectal twist to an already existing study, the chances of finding appropriate images that are controlled and balanced for all related factors is extremely slim. In such cases, it's helpful if you possess art or photography skills. Not artistically inclined? In some labs, members help each other out by swapping skills in stimulus creation (e.g., experimenter #1 might serve as the stimulus voice for experimenter #2, who helped draw stimuli for an experiment run by experimenter #1).

Audio-visual stimuli are, as the name would suggest, stimuli that incorporate both sounds and images. Video is the most common form of audio-visual stimuli. Working with audio-visual stimuli is complicated because you need to control (or balance) all of the factors that arise from using auditory stimuli as well as those that arise from using visual stimuli.

Another common stimulus type is **text**, which includes written words, sentences, and passages. Two things to keep in mind when selecting text stimuli are the length of the items and the potential salience of rare letters (e.g., the letter x) that might draw attention.

It is worth noting that text is processed differently from images; for example, there is evidence that, compared to images, text results in faster activation of the phoneme level (Huettig & McQueen 2007). Thus, text shouldn't necessarily be treated as identical to images in sociolinguistic experiments. We don't know enough yet about how social information might interact with different types of stimuli. That can be frustrating because it means that sometimes you might have to learn the hard way. On the other hand, there are a number of theoretical and methodological questions here just waiting to be explored.

Since you should control anything and everything that can vary and might influence responses, there's a whole lot you need to consider. This is one reason that the best way to get into experimental work is to base the first version of your experiment on an existing one. The study you replicate should be one that inspires you. I also recommend that you choose one that was published in a journal that caters to experimentalists; this way, you know that, during the review process, the work was reviewed by scholars who specialize in experimental methodologies and it is, therefore, more likely to be methodologically sound. Journals such as *Journal of Memory and Language* and *Cognition* have high standards for experimental work and would be a good place to look for examples of studies to emulate.

2.1.2. What to measure

When designing an experiment, one of the first things that needs to be decided is what to measure. That is, what is the dependent variable? One possibility is to look at reaction times (how long it takes the participant to respond to a stimulus) or a response (did they answer A or B), or maybe it's best to measure something from the participant's speech, such as vowel formants or the likelihood of producing a syntactic structure. The answer to what you should measure, of course, depends on your research question. The simplest experiments in terms of their design are those that elicit the most natural styles of speech, like conversation. This is because the more natural the medium of the data (i.e., conversation > reading passage > wordlist > forced-choice response), the fewer the factors it's possible to control (i.e., conversation < reading passage < wordlist < forced-choice response). This is not to say that a study using conversational data is easier than a study using forced-choice responses – conversational data are usually very difficult and time-consuming to analyze – but there are fewer factors that can be controlled, which means the design can be much simpler.

Responses that are based on time (e.g., response times and eye-tracking data) require the greatest amount of control. Special considerations must be taken into account when collecting these types of data. My advice: unless you are working very closely with a researcher who has extensive experience using reaction times or eye-tracking data, do not begin your foray into experimental work by using one of these as your dependent variable. That said, they are important to understand, so I begin this section with talking about the dependent variables that require the most control (i.e., reaction time data) and then move on to those that require less.

Reaction times

Reaction times are a measurement of the duration between a stimulus and a response. They are a type of dependent variable that is **continuous**, meaning that they are numeric and there are a large (hypothetically infinite) number of possible durations. By measuring reaction times, researchers can investigate differences that are subtler than those that might arise looking only at responses. There are a number of factors that might cause slower reaction times in one condition than another, such as a greater amount of planning pre-production, more competition from similar-sounding words, or a heavier cognitive load due to greater stress on working memory. With more difficult tasks, you can expect longer reaction times. But other stuff – like an auditory stimulus produced with a slow speech rate or a participant who is being especially careful – can also induce slower reaction times. Reaction times are a powerful tool because they can reveal variation that is subtler than that which could be examined using responses. But this subtlety also means that they are easily affected by a wide range of factors, and these factors must be controlled in order for the results to be meaningful.

Should you decide to collect reaction times, it's important that you have the correct tools. Reaction times should not be collected using a keyboard due to inaccuracy of the temporal data logged by the computer. Instead, a button box (for a click response) or a voice key (for an oral response) should be used since these provide more accurate time measurements. Investing in these tools is well worth the expense. An inexpensive alternative is to use a recorder, collecting an audible cue for the stimulus and an oral response from the participant. The duration between them can later be measured and treated as the dependent variable.

Before running the experiment, all stimuli should be normed so that all factors that could influence response times are controlled across conditions (see Section 2.1.1). It is always a good idea to norm stimuli, but it's especially important if you're working with reaction times. The time between stimuli (known as interstimulus intervals, or ISIs) should also be considered; be sure to consult previous work that uses the same paradigm. Because there are so many different factors that can influence the time it takes to respond, it's important to control everything that's possible to control for in the stimuli and to balance anything that cannot be controlled.

Even after everything has been considered for set-up of the experiment, there are a number of things to keep in mind for the analysis of reaction times. First, the researcher must decide the appropriate time course for the measurement: does it make sense to measure from the beginning of the stimulus, from the end of it, or from some disambiguation point during it? Most commonly, researchers measure from the disambiguation point, or – if there are different predictions for the different time points – at multiple points during the stimulus. Then, the researcher needs to decide whether the reaction times need to be normalized in some way to account for differences across subjects or items. Residual reaction times can be calculated from the raw reaction times in order to statistically account for variability among individual participants in how they are affected by traits of the stimuli that are non-critical for the research question. These commonly include durational factors, such as the number of syllables or letters. These questions should be considered during the design stage since the answers may help inform the design. See Chapter 3 for examples of tasks that can be used to elicit reaction times and a discussion of considerations to keep in mind when designing the tasks.

> ## What's that?
>
> Remember, a **dependent variable** is a factor that varies and the variation is hypothesized to be influenced by or linked to one or more **independent variables**, which are sometimes referred to as **predicting variables**.
>
> A **continuous variable** is a numeric variable such as time that is infinite in either direction or – if bounded – can be divided into infinitely smaller components.
>
> A **categorical variable** or a **discrete variable** is a variable that has discrete categories, referred to as **levels**.
>
> A **nominal variable** is a type categorical variable in which the levels are not ranked. An example is the participant's regional background.
>
> An **ordered variable** is a type of categorical variable with levels that are ranked. One example is ratings from a rating task. The dependent variable from a rating task is not continuous because the values are not absolute; while 'very much', 'neutral', and 'not really' might be coded as 1, 2, and 3, 'very much' doesn't equal half what 'neutral' equals, and the levels are not necessarily equidistant.
>
> An **interval variable** is like an ordered variable except that the difference between the intervals is meaningful. Most sociolinguistic variables that appear to be interval variables are in fact ordered.

Forced-choice responses

Luckily, not all experiments are as tricky to set up as those that collect reaction times. Control and balance are, of course, important for all experiments, but responses are usually not as susceptible to influence as are reaction times. If planning to analyze responses, it is important that there is variation in the responses; if measuring accuracy, for example, it cannot be at ceiling. (Accuracy is at ceiling when participants are at or near 100% accuracy, so there is a "ceiling" keeping them from improving any further.) This means, in turn, that not all tasks are appropriate for collecting responses, but there are plenty to choose from and it is from among these tasks that I recommend that those who are new to experimental methods begin to hone their experiment design skills.

One of the most straightforward types of experimental data to collect and analyze are forced-choice responses. The simplest is a binary forced-choice task, where participants are given two possible answers from which they choose one, resulting in a binary, **discrete factor** for analysis. A larger number of options can also be provided but this complicates both the design and the analysis. Similarly, it's possible to provide choices that either do not require a response or allow participants to select more than one. Doing this makes statistical analysis more difficult, so it is most commonly done in preliminary work that is used to inform the design of later (forced-choice) experiments.

Rating tasks are also a type of forced-choice response. Rather than providing discrete categories to choose from, rating tasks allow participants to respond on a scale or continuum, resulting in an **ordered variable** (i.e., while technically numeric, the variable is not truly continuous). Rating tasks are discussed in detail in Section 3.1.1.

Open-ended responses

Open-ended responses are rich in information. In tasks that collect open-ended responses, no responses are provided by the researcher; instead, participants respond to a stimulus in their own words. Open-ended questions are normally asked, but more pointed questions or requests (e.g., *Please list three words that you feel best describe what this speaker might look like*) can also be used. Due to the richness of the data, results can be revealing, especially for studies examining listeners' language stereotypes or listeners' perceptions of speaker style. Analyzing the data, however, can be difficult, and statistical analysis often does not yield robust results. Thus, open-ended responses are normally used to inform trends observed in production or to aid in the design of subsequent experiments.

Linguistic variables

In many sociolinguistic studies, a linguistic variable serves as the dependent variable. This is also true of experimental work, particularly that

Explore the methods

Studies on the companion website that use these stimulus types are:
reaction times
Kim (2016)
binary forced-choice questions
Squires (2013a)
Yu and Lee (2014)
ratings on a scale
Levon (2007)
open-ended responses
Drager, Hardeman Guthrie, Schutz, and Chik (in prep)

which focuses on production data. Using linguistic variables as the dependent variable is appropriate for research questions that focus on differences in speakers' production. Experiments along these lines can be used to investigate variation at any level of the grammar.

There are several other types of data (e.g., written translations, fill in the blank) that can be collected in sociolinguistic experiments, but these are much less common and are discussed in the relevant sections of Chapters 3, 4, and 5.

2.1.3. Disguising the hypothesis

Most often in experimental work the researcher wants to disguise their specific hypothesis so that participants' responses aren't influenced by trying to respond in a certain way, such as how they think the researcher wants them to respond. There are a number of techniques that are used for this purpose:

- vagueness in language used to describe the study
- misleading instructions (note that this constitutes deception; see Section 2.3)
- asking questions in a way that do not lead participants
- use of distractor stimuli or tasks (fillers)

When describing the study so that participants can determine whether or not they want to participate, it is important to use language that the participant can understand (e.g., don't go spouting off about vowel formants) and give enough information that they can make their decision. It is also important that participants are not made aware of the specific hypothesis, unless that is a part of the study's design. In some cases, deception is used when describing a study or when giving instructions, telling participants that the research is about something entirely different from what it is actually about. When this is done, it is imperative that – after the participant has completed the tasks – they are informed about the actual purpose of the experiment and are given the opportunity to rescind their original consent.

The ways in which questions are asked can also influence responses and, in some cases, may reveal the hypothesis. Take care that the wording used in the questions does neither. For example, in a recent survey distributed by the Republican Party in the United States (https://gop.com/mainstream-media-accountability-survey/), survey respondents were asked "Do you believe that the mainstream media does not do their due diligence fact-checking before publishing stories on the Trump administration?" Intentionally or not, the wording used in this question (as well as the rest of the survey questions) reveals the biases of those administering the survey and, as such, is a good example of a poorly designed survey question.

Fillers (also known as distractors) are stimuli that are used to hide the specific hypothesis being tested. Thus, while participants in an eye-tracking experiment will be aware that the speed of their shifting gaze is being studied and that there are certain stimuli that share specific characteristics, the inclusion of fillers helps to disguise the specific linguistic and social factors being studied. Filler tasks can also be used, and are especially useful in cases when the main task is repetitive and boring. Responses to filler items and tasks are not normally analyzed since their primary purpose is to distract the participant. However, sometimes they can reveal participants who are behaving strangely, and they can also sometimes be used to provide pilot data (or even primary data) for another project. Adding this layer makes the experiment more difficult and time-consuming to set up, but it can save time in the long run. However, the main experiment should remain the focus during the design phase; do not use fillers as test items for another experiment if doing so puts the primary experiment in jeopardy by, for example, introducing an undesirable prime (see Section 2.1.7 for a discussion of priming).

When disguising the hypothesis, take care that the experiment does not get too long. Difficult or especially repetitive (i.e., boring) tasks should be kept as short as possible (15 minutes is good). More engaging experiments can take up to an hour, but participants may express feeling fatigued if the experiment goes longer. If necessary, participants can be offered breaks but care should be taken to ensure that they are not being exposed to an undesirable prime during their break (e.g., closing their eyes for a minute or standing up to stretch would be ok, but checking their phone or social media would not.)

Depending on the difficulty of the experiment, it can be a good idea to include some questions that have easy answers, so that the participants don't always feel like they're guessing. Such questions can serve as additional distractors and can also serve as a kind of safeguard to help identify participants who are not taking the task seriously or are having trouble with the task for some other reason, such as sounds being played at too low a volume.

2.1.4. Item repetition

You may have noticed that, for some experiments, participants respond to a single stimulus item two or more times over the course of the experiment.

Repetition should be avoided if it's not necessary. There are two main reasons, however, that it may be needed. The first is that repetition allows the researcher to test for consistency within the responses of individual participants. Another is that repetition provides more statistical power, which is especially important to consider if there are a limited number of distinct items that meet your stimulus specifications (i.e., you're lacking power in the number of items so you make up for it through using repetition) or there are too few participants who meet your participant requirements. If items repeat in your experiment for any reason, it's important to consider the repetition during analysis since participants' behavior can shift as a result of the repetition.

2.1.5. Randomization

The order in which stimuli are presented can affect participant behavior on a task. In addition, a participant's response strategy may shift over the course of the experiment as they become familiarized or bored with the task. While this cannot be overcome, **randomizing** the tokens means that we can be sure that any consistent differences observed across test items are not due to the order in which the items are presented. Tokens are fully randomized when they are presented in a random order that differs for every participant. However, this is not always desirable because, for example, if two similar items are played consecutively, it would likely influence results. In these cases, a pseudorandom order is used, in which certain restrictions are placed on the presentation order, and the order varies randomly within those set parameters.

2.1.6. Counterbalancing and Latin Square design

Participants often change behavior on a task over time as a result of learning or boredom. To avoid such effects influencing the interpretation of data collected using a within-subjects design, it is important to **counterbalance** the conditions. To counterbalance the conditions, the order of the conditions should vary across different groups of participants. An example is shown in Table 2.1, with a sketch on the left and an example with stimulus names on the right. The different orders are referred to as lists. You'll notice that specific lexical items (e.g., *cat*) occur with one of the conditions in List 1 and with a different condition in List 2. Alternatively, it may be desirable to block by condition; counterbalancing should also

Table 2.1 Example of counterbalancing with two conditions, shown in a sketch on the left and shown with stimuli from a matched-guise experiment on the right

Sketch			Example with stimuli		
Item	List 1	List 2	Item	List 1	List 2
1	Cond 1	Cond 2	cat	cat-guise1	cat-guise2
2	Cond 2	Cond 1	fat	fat-guise2	fat-guise1
3	Cond 1	Cond 2	sat	sat-guise1	sat-guise2
4	Cond 2	Cond 1	mat	mat-guise2	mat-guise1
5	Cond 1	Cond 2	hat	hat-guise1	hat-guise2
6	Cond 2	Cond 1	bat	bat-guise2	bat-guise1
7	Cond 1	Cond 2	sat	sat-guise1	sat-guise2
8	Cond 2	Cond 1	pat	pat-guise2	pat-guise1
9	Cond 1	Cond 2	rat	rat-guise1	rat-guise2
10	Cond 2	Cond 1	gnat	gnat-guise2	gnat-guise1

be used in such cases. One thing to keep in mind regardless is that, when counterbalancing, all possible combinations of factors should be balanced across conditions.

Full counterbalancing is rarely used for experiments with more than three test factors. This is because of the increasingly large number of lists that would need to be produced. To demonstrate this, the example from Table 2.1 is shown in Table 2.2 with three conditions instead of two. The number of lists is determined by a factorial of the number of conditions. This means that a design with four conditions would have 24 lists (i.e., $4! = 4 \times 3 \times 2 \times 1 = 24$).

Therefore, in such cases, it's more common for researchers to adopt a **Latin Square** design. With a Latin Square, the number of lists is considerably reduced because each condition is "bumped down" by one across each list, as shown in Table 2.3. (If you don't see what I mean, try highlighting the cells, one color for each condition. You'll soon see the pattern.)

Using a Latin Square dramatically reduces the number of lists. And while it doesn't completely eradicate the possibility of order effects, it makes them much less likely, so the cost-benefit tradeoff is usually weighed in their favor.

Table 2.2 Example of counterbalancing with three conditions

Item	List 1	List 2	List 3	List 4	List 5	List 6
1	Cond 1	Cond 1	Cond 2	Cond 2	Cond 3	Cond 3
2	Cond 2	Cond 3	Cond 3	Cond 1	Cond 1	Cond 2
3	Cond 3	Cond 2	Cond 1	Cond 3	Cond 2	Cond 1
4	Cond 1	Cond 1	Cond 2	Cond 2	Cond 3	Cond 3
5	Cond 2	Cond 3	Cond 3	Cond 1	Cond 1	Cond 2
6	Cond 3	Cond 2	Cond 1	Cond 3	Cond 2	Cond 1
7	Cond 1	Cond 1	Cond 2	Cond 2	Cond 3	Cond 3
8	Cond 2	Cond 3	Cond 3	Cond 1	Cond 1	Cond 2
9	Cond 3	Cond 2	Cond 1	Cond 3	Cond 2	Cond 1

Table 2.3 Example showing a Latin Square

Item	List 1	List 2	List 3
1	Cond 1	Cond 3	Cond 2
2	Cond 2	Cond 1	Cond 3
3	Cond 3	Cond 2	Cond 1
4	Cond 1	Cond 3	Cond 2
5	Cond 2	Cond 1	Cond 3
6	Cond 3	Cond 2	Cond 1
7	Cond 1	Cond 3	Cond 2
8	Cond 2	Cond 1	Cond 3
9	Cond 3	Cond 2	Cond 1

2.1.7. Priming

Many experiments use **priming** to test a hypothesis. Priming occurs when exposure to one stimulus affects subsequent behavior. For example, upon hearing the word 'flower', associated words, such as 'daisy', are comprehended and responded to more quickly. This type of priming is known as semantic priming. There are a large number of experimental paradigms that rely on priming and an even larger number where priming can optionally be used. Priming can be used to explore both production and perception, and there is also little restriction on data type: priming can be used when collecting binary responses, open-ended responses, reaction times, eye movements, and more.

In addition to semantic priming, priming can occur with phonetic forms: people are generally faster at understanding a word when it is repeated by the same speaker than when it is repeated by a novel speaker. And priming can occur with lexical forms, so that participants are faster at responding to non-novel words. Within-modal priming can be used, where, for example, an auditory prime can be used to prime an auditory target. Alternatively, a cross-modal priming paradigm can be used, where the prime is, for example, an auditory token and the target is visually presented.

Of special interest to sociolinguists are social primes, where social characteristics, styles, and socially linked concepts can prime associated linguistic forms, influencing production and perception. There is less work in this area than with other forms of priming, making it an excellent avenue to explore.

In many studies that use priming, it is important to establish a baseline. This means that the researcher can get an idea of how a participant behaves when not exposed to a prime. This can be done by including a condition without any prime or with a neutral prime (e.g., a shape or silhouette). For some factors, baselines will not be possible. In particular, this is true for social factors; since a neutral option is not possible, responses are subject to the participants' prejudices and social biases. And without knowing the full extent of what these might be, it can make interpreting the outcome tricky. Thus, the researcher may instead wish to seize control of participants' social biases through exposure to socially relevant primes, comparing differences in behavior across the priming conditions. In cases where a "neutral" condition is used, two test conditions should be used as well. The test conditions should be predicted to influence shifts in the opposite direction from one another, with the baseline predicted to fall between them. Then, if no difference is observed between test conditions, there is a null effect, regardless of any differences between one of the tests and the baseline. Remember, the baseline when working with social primes is something of a black box, rendering it fairly meaningless for the hypothesis being tested if it doesn't fall between the two test conditions. In some cases, it may overlap with one of the test conditions, which can be informative as to the participants' underlying biases.

> ## What's that?
>
> Experimental **fillers** are stimulus items that are included in order to disguise the hypothesis.
>
> When **randomization** is used, it means there is a different, randomly determined order of items for each participant.
>
> **Counterbalancing** is balancing that occurs across different portions of the experiment in order to offset order effects.
>
> A **Latin Square design** is a method of counterbalancing that requires fewer lists than would be required by a fully counterbalanced design.

2.1.8. Effects from the experimenter, location, and other potential primes

The identity of the experimenter can influence participant behavior on both production and perception tasks. Thus, experimenter identity needs to either be controlled (i.e., the same person collects all of the data and does their best to interact with each participant in the same way) or it needs to be balanced appropriately as with any other factor (see Section 2.1.6). Even in cases when a single experimenter is used, who they are and how they might vary when interacting with different participants should be considered.

In addition to the experimenter, the location in which the experiment is run should be controlled since this, too, can influence behavior. Some of the differences may be related to differences in noise in the different locations (inducing a Lombard-like effect with shifts in realization that are characteristic of speech produced in noise) or differences in familiarity and comfort (inducing unintended shifts across participants).

Finally, even objects in the room can affect behavior. Care must be taken to control everything that is within the experimenter's power to control.

2.1.9. Experimental software: in the lab, in the field, and online

There are a number of different experiment-running software packages available. In this section, I outline the advantages and disadvantages of commonly used software to help you decide which one is best for you.

The most commonly used software is E-Prime. E-Prime is extremely powerful and can be used for almost all of the methods described in

Chapters 3 and 4. It is extremely well documented, and there are a number of tutorials freely available online. In addition, they have support staff available. The biggest disadvantage is the cost. Lab-based licenses can be purchased, but an additional fee must then be paid for any of that lab's laptops to be used during fieldwork that involves changes to the design or implementation while away from the lab. Another potential disadvantage is that its use is restricted to Windows machines.

A free, open-access, platform-independent option is PsychoPy. PsychoPy has not yet been developed to do everything that E-Prime can do, but it's free and relatively easy to use. It's also Python based, so anyone with Python skills can develop it to fit their needs.

Increasingly, researchers have been running online experiments. The advantages are, of course, the smaller amount of time spent on data collection and the convenience for participants, which makes recruitment easier. However, the drawbacks are a lack of control over a number of factors, including attention to the task, the presence of other people in the room, the use of headphones, and the location. Thus, I am generally not a proponent of online experiments unless they are conducted to inform the design or interpretation of another study and the results are highly consistent with the hypotheses.

There are a few different options for running an experiment online. While many labs develop in-house software to run their online experiments, other options include Experigen (Becker & Levine 2013), PsyToolkit, jsPysch, and oTree.

Explore the methods

Examples of materials used to run experiments in the platforms below can be found on the companion website: https://www.bloomsbury.com/cw/experimental-research-methods-in-sociolinguistics/

E-Prime

Walker and Campbell-Kibler (2015)

Experigen

Levon (2007, 2014)

In addition, a handout and sample from a 2014 NWAV workshop on experimental methods is provided in the materials for this chapter.

2.1.10. Headphones or not?

The preferred method for perception tasks is to play the sounds over headphones rather than, say, over computer speakers. Headphones provide superior sound quality and help mask background noise stemming from the experimental environment (e.g., hum from lights or a computer) and are, therefore, highly recommended for research questions that involve phonetics.

When selecting headphones, quality is important. Cheap headphones should be avoided. Circumaural (i.e., the kind that go all the way around the ear to touch the head) and supra-aural (the kind that touches the ear) provide the clearest sound. At this time, there are no known negative consequences of using noise-canceling headphones for collecting perception data, so these may also be desirable, especially if working in a location with a large amount of background noise. However, many noise-canceling headphones must be switched on for their noise-canceling properties to work, so using them adds one more thing to remember when meeting with participants. Also, these headphones rely on batteries (batteries that tend to run out quickly!), so fresh batteries should be kept on hand.

Before running an experiment, sound volume should be checked, and if the room and/or equipment is used for purposes other than running the experiment, the volume should be checked prior to every participant. Ensure the sound is played at a comfortable level for the participants. For excellent sound quality, it can be worthwhile to invest in a good amplifier rather than relying on the defaults in the computer hardware.

2.1.11. Practice tasks

Before they begin the task, it's often a good idea to give participants a chance to try the task. But when is a practice test needed? It's a good idea to include a practice task if you're collecting data that depends on time, like reaction times, eye-tracking, or mouse-tracking data. That way, you won't end up with a bunch of slow reaction times just because participants were trying to figure out the task. But even if you're collecting responses, it can be a good idea to include a practice task, especially if the experiment involves a task that might be weird or confusing, or if some training is required. For example, phoneme monitoring tasks are weird to participants because they rely on people using their ears (listening for phonemes) rather than their eyes (relying on spelling) but most participants are used to thinking about language in terms of letters rather than sounds. So, if using this type of task or some other task that may be counter-intuitive to some participants, it's a good idea to use a practice task that gives feedback to participants about whether they responded accurately and, if not, why. Just make sure that the sounds and words (and, if relevant, voices) used during the practice task are not the same as those used during the main experiment.

When is a practice test *unnecessary*? In some cases, the experimental task is a straightforward one, such as a reading task or one that, when given a scenario, simply involves talking about it. If including a practice task doesn't make it easier for your participants or doesn't garner better data for your purposes, then there isn't any reason to include it.

One thing to keep in mind when setting up the practice task is that the goal is to clarify the task that they'll be doing without making your data unusable. So be careful that you:

- DON'T give away whatever it is that you're looking at.
- Instead, it can work well to choose practice stimuli that are similar to your filler items. This can help distract participants away from your specific hypothesis.
- DON'T expose the participants to any critical stimuli before the experiment begins.
- Instead, choose new items that don't appear elsewhere in the experiment.
- DON'T unintentionally prime the participants.
- Instead, include practice items that will not influence responses to your test variables. For sociolinguists, this means considering both linguistic priming (e.g., don't include the word *nurse* in the practice task if *doctor* is a test item) and social priming (e.g., use a different voice from that used in the main experiment and/or consider the link between words in the practice task and social factors being tested).

This may seem like a lot to think about at first, but it really does get easier the more times you do it.

2.2. Recruiting participants

It probably goes without saying that recruiting participants is usually easier if you can pay them. However, many people simply don't have the money to pay participants and I am, unfortunately, among those without research funds. Fortunately, this means I have a lot of experience recruiting participants without paying them, and I'm happy to share my methods with you.

The first (and least successful) method involves approaching people who you've never met and asking them to take part. This method is difficult (especially with tasks that don't involve chatting with someone) because most people say "no" and that can get disheartening when it happens over and over and over again. However, every so often, someone will say "yes." If you find someone who is willing to take part and you give the would-be participant your contact details, you will likely never hear from them again. However, if you have a mobile experiment, you can bring it with you and they can do it right then and there. If the experiment needs to take place in a lab or other predetermined setting, I would suggest immediately setting up a day and time to meet. Also, be sure to get their contact details so that you can remind them about the appointment ahead of time and, if they are a no-show, you can follow-up. (If that happens, be sure to be nice! Remember, they're not as obsessed with your experiment as you are, and they could have easily forgotten.)

The second method is recruitment through using, for example, individual small rewards (e.g., candy bars) or raffle tickets for a large reward (e.g., a $50 gift certificate). In some places, I've had a lot of luck with chocolate as an incentive, but this doesn't work everywhere or for everyone. To get the word out about the experiment (and any delicious reward), posters and social media can be used to provide a short description of the task and your contact details.

The third method is through word-of-mouth or the snowball method, where every person who takes part suggests a few other people who might want to participate. One drawback of this method is that you won't end up with anything close to a random sample, even one that's necessarily representative of the community you intend to study. However, this method can work quite well for a lot of sociolinguistic work, especially that which focuses on specific communities of practice or social networks.

The fourth method is through an online tool, such as Mechanical Turk, that collects responses and pays participants a nominal sum. While not technically free, it can be a way to spend very little but get a whole lot of data. The tools that can be used this way vary by country and are changing all the time, so I recommend spending a little bit of time exploring the different options before proceeding. Also, there are some valid concerns with online experiments (see Section 2.1.9).

The final method is through a participant pool. The benefit of using a participant pool is that it's relatively easy to recruit participants since most participant pools are a way for students to get partial course credit in exchange for taking part. And, as someone who learned about a range of experimental paradigms by taking part in a variety of experiments from different departments, I can attest that it can be a good experience for student-participants, too. One drawback of participant pools is that your target population (e.g., native speakers of a specific language who are living in diaspora) may be too small a percentage of the student body for the participant pool to be very useful to answer your research question. Another drawback is that this is a non-random sample and university students probably behave differently than non-students on a variety of tasks, especially if they are students of Linguistics.

Recruiting participants brings up important questions about ethics in data collection, which brings me to the next topic: ethics.

2.3. Ethics in experimental work

Unfortunately, there have been cases where researchers have acted unethically, so it's important to talk about the rights and wrongs of doing research so that you can avoid unethical pitfalls. Here, I will discuss three main areas with which we are concerned: what is ethical during data collection, what is ethical during data storage, and what is ethical when reporting results. For a discussion of deception, please see Section 2.1.3.

2.3.1. Ethics during data collection

One ethical concern during data collection is the power dynamic between the researcher and the participant. If the researcher has more power in the relationship (like a professor with a student, or a CEO and their employee), the participant may feel coerced into taking part in the experiment, and coercion is considered unethical. *I ran an experiment with students. Does that mean I acted unethically?* Not necessarily. If the experiment was for teaching rather than research, then there's no problem, assuming there was minimal risk and pain (beyond boredom) from taking part. I use fake experiments with my students all time to teach them about experimental methods and data, and the responses are only for class purposes. *The experiment was not exclusively for teaching. So did I act unethically?* Still, not necessarily. (Here's where it gets tricky.) If the students felt coerced into taking the experiment – they weren't given a variety of options and participation affected their grade in some way or they were led to believe it would – then we have a problem. *So how in the world are participant pools ethical if students receive partial class credit for taking part in an experiment?* Well, most participant pools are used for a variety of different projects, and students can choose among the projects to decide which one(s) they take part in. As an extra anti-coercion measure, instructors can offer alternative ways for students to fulfill the requirement, such as reporting on select documentaries, writing a review of a selected article, or doing some data collection in the community (e.g., photographs for a linguistic landscape project). In addition, participation can be provided as extra credit, making it non-obligatory. When I include participation in an experiment as an option to receive course credit, I make sure students know that it makes no difference to me whether they take part in an experiment or fulfill the requirement through some other means, such as watching a documentary. And if it's a semester when I'm collecting data using the participant pool, I ask students in my class who want to participate in an experiment to take part in someone else's, just so I can be sure that none of them feels coerced.

Another concern during data collection is the risk to the participant. While the vast majority of experimental work in sociolinguistics involves minimal risk, there are some exceptions. Sociolinguists interested in emotions, attitudes, and taboo topics or incriminating behavior need to take extra precautions for data collection, storage, and dissemination. In some cases, including a trigger warning for any delicate topics may be necessary, and researchers should have a plan on hand (including contact details of health professionals) should the participant exhibit signs of distress.

Researchers working with vulnerable populations also need to take extra precautions. Vulnerable populations include minors, pregnant women, prisoners, people suffering from a mental illness, people with cognitive or physical disabilities, and people who are economically or educationally disadvantaged. Members of these groups may be more vulnerable to coercion, due to influence from, for example, a parent or doctor. Thus, assuming you get the necessary consent (from a parent/guardian) and assent (from the child), it is ethical to run an experiment on a three-year old if your research question is about first language acquisition and the experiment involves minimal risk to the child. In contrast, it is unethical to run your experiment with a vulnerable population just because you think it will be easy to get them to do the experiment. Should the involvement of people from that population be critical to the study, precautions need to be taken in order to ensure that none of the subjects is coerced into taking part.

2.3.2. Ethical considerations for data storage

Compared with some other kinds of sociolinguistic data, the ethical storage of data is generally less of a concern with experimental sociolinguistic data since it is most often completely anonymized and the content of the data is usually as mundane as whether or not someone produced a word with a raised vowel. There are, however, some exceptions. For example, if someone is running an experiment with responses from a small community of practice, the identity of the participant is probably a critical component of the study, so the data may not be completely anonymized. Alternatively, the researcher might collect data that has a sensitive topic or that could be potentially embarrassing if responses and non-anonymized identifiers were released to the public. When responses cannot be anonymized or when the content could negatively impact the participant, the security of how the data are stored is normally increased. For example, data may need to be stored on password-protected data-bases, and sharing the data may be restricted.

2.3.3. Ethics in reporting results

Because experimental data is normally quantitative and completely anonymized, the ethical considerations that must be made in other types of sociolinguistic work (e.g., ethnography) are less frequently relevant. But that's not to say it's impossible. A good rule of thumb: if it could hurt the participant, don't publish it.

2.4. Publishing work in experimental sociolinguistics

Despite the long history of experimental work in sociolinguistics, it is not always easy to publish such work in a sociolinguistics journal. This may be partly due to the methods, but it is also linked with the types of cross-disciplinary research questions that tend to drive work along these lines. Luckily, there are plenty of excellent general linguistics journals that happily accept papers reporting results from experimental sociolinguistics, and – for research questions that span subdisciplines – these may be the most appropriate venues anyway. At this point in time, there is no journal that is primarily focused on experimental work in sociolinguistics. However, a new journal on sociophonetics, *Revista Letras de Hoje*, may help fill this niche for the more phonetically inclined. As more and more sociolinguists employ experimental methods and as the value of such work is more widely accepted, we're likely to see a greater number of journals that cater to those of us who are interested in these questions and methods; in fact, it already seems to be changing. To identify appropriate venues, I suggest perusing the journals that published the work presented in this book, focusing especially on those that have informed your work.

2.5. Chapter summary

In this chapter, I present some of the many aspects of experimental design that need to be considered prior to setting up an experiment. These include the importance of:

- control
- proper balancing techniques
- fillers
- practice tasks

Also discussed are the many different kinds of stimuli that can be used, the many different kinds of primes, and how to follow ethical practices for participant recruitment, data collection, and reporting results.

Main points

- Control is important.
- When complete counterbalancing introduces too many lists, a Latin Square design can be used.
- While there is a lot involved in designing an experiment, it gets easier with experience.
- Start simple.
- Act ethically.

Further reading

Martin, David W. (1996). *Doing Psychology Experiments,* 4th edition. Pacific Grove, CA: Brooks/Cole.

Experimental designs to examine perception

3

The study of perception seems intimidating at first. Once you understand how to approach it, though, you'll see that it isn't so daunting after all.

– Erik Thomas (2011: 55)

Many of the perception studies discussed in Chapter 1 build on work from experimental phonetics/phonology and social psychology, combining various approaches when appropriate. As a researcher, you don't need to become an expert with every single one of the methods, but it's helpful to be familiar with the wide range of paradigms so that you can be sure to use the most appropriate method for your research question.

In experimental sociolinguistics, there are two types of research questions: those that build on our understanding of society and social factors, and those that expand our knowledge of how linguistic information is represented and processed (see Hazen 2014). In this chapter, I first step through experimental paradigms that are especially well suited to investigate the more socially focused research questions in Section 3.1, and then in Section 3.2, I turn to those that are used to examine the cognitive aspects of linguistic structure.

3.1. A focus on the social

If you answer a call from an unfamiliar person, you usually don't know very much about them before you hear them speak. However, as soon as they talk, you might know (or believe you know) something about their gender, where they are from, what their ethnicity might be, or how tall they are. People even make inferences about hairstyles, clothes, and favorite activities based on nothing more than the way someone sounds.

There are a number of different research questions that delve into the phenomenon of person perception, exploring the ways in which language influences characteristics attributed to the talker. The questions include: How accurate are the perceptions? What kind of prejudiced behavior might result from the listeners' perceptions, and what are the real-world implications for the speakers? What is it about language that listeners tune into to make these inferences? What kinds of linguistic cues are responded to more positively than others? And how, cognitively, do people do this based on nothing more than a voice?

The link between language and person perception relates to language stereotypes. Language stereotypes, like all stereotypes, can be positive or negative. Individuals can be aware they have the stereotype, but they also might not be aware of it. Or they might be aware of it but deny that it exists and try their best to hide it. (This is especially true of negative stereotypes.) This can make studying the stereotypes tricky: if people don't want to admit having them, how can you study them?

In this section, we'll first step through experimental methods that can be used to investigate explicit associations (which are good for investigating stereotypes that people don't mind sharing) and then we'll get to those that are used to examine implicit associations (which may be better for examining those that people don't want to own up to). It's up to the researcher to decide which method is most appropriate for their research question, with consideration given to the aspect of language being investigated and the community from which participants will be recruited. Often, it's a good idea to use more than one method so that you can understand perception from a variety of different angles. The use of multiple methods to get at the answer to a question is known as *triangulation.*

Something to keep in mind when designing this type of experiment is that there are separate effects that arise from sociolinguistic indices and processing speed. Processing speed is known to affect the perception of a number of different traits (e.g., credibility). For example, as demonstrated by Lev-Ari and Keysar (2010), when a voice takes longer to process, it will often be evaluated as less credible, and this effect can arise even if there is no a priori negative association with the voice. Therefore, an effect of a stimulus on a perceived trait does not necessarily mean that the linguistic cues in the signal are socially indexed with the trait. So, if you want to investigate socio-indexical relationships – particularly those involving social traits that are influenced by processing speed – proper norming of stimuli is necessary in order to control the speed at which the stimuli are processed. (This involves setting up a simple task to check that, across conditions, there is no difference in processing speed.) In addition, other tasks and/or stimuli can be included to test the extent to which listener evaluations are influenced by processing speed. For example, if interested in whether negative evaluations of L2 speech arise from negative stereotypes of L2 speakers versus slower processing time of L2 speech, tokens of L1 speech covered in noise (to increase processing time) can be included to help interpret the listeners' responses to the L2 talker.

What's that?

Person perception refers to the amalgamation of visual and non-visual characteristics attributed to an unseen and, often, unfamiliar speaker.

When researchers use **triangulation**, they adopt three (or more) distinct methods to address a single research question.

3.1.1. Rating tasks

To investigate questions about how language influences person perception, researchers have most often used a rating task. In a rating task, listeners are asked to listen to a stimulus and use a scale to respond. In some cases, the scale is one of affirmation (Example 3.1a). Other scales have choices at the endpoints that are assumed to be opposite ends of a continuum (Example 3.1b). Different researchers select various numbers of points along their scale, depending on the degree of differentiation between the choices that they want to provide to participants. Some researchers prefer to use an even number of choices in order to force participants to "choose a side"; this has the benefit of simplifying analysis because the responses can be treated as binary (agree vs. disagree). However, there are some downsides to this method: participants might not like it if there's no neutral item, and it might be important to distinguish those items that are non-polarizing from those that are. Providing a neutral response is an especially good idea if the scale is constructed so that the endpoints are opposites (e.g., agree/disagree). A neutral item is less necessary when the endpoints are from one extreme to a more neutral position (e.g., wonderful/fine). My recommendation is to use a neutral item in your norming and/or pilot study. Based on the responses you observe, you can decide whether the main experiment should include one and what the appropriate endpoints of the scale are.

(3.1)

    a) This speaker is often silly.
        completely agree—kind of agree—no opinion—disagree—strongly disagree

    b) This speaker is:
        very attractive—a little attractive—not attractive and not ugly—ugly—very ugly

    c) This person would do a _____ job as a newscaster.
        wonderful—great—good—fine

Did you notice how in Example 3.1, the various points of the scale are labeled? This is known as anchoring. At a minimum, you should provide labels for the endpoints, but labels for each point are recommended if they add clarity for the participant in terms of how to interpret the scale. Wells and Smith (1960) found that ratings are more reliable when every point is labeled. Because different participants may have different understandings of what the labels mean and because, when beginning the experiment, they don't yet know the range they will use (and are therefore unlikely to use the endpoints early on in the experiment), properly anchoring the points requires an explanation. The easiest way to do this is to provide a token that is stimulus-like for each end of the continuum prior to beginning the actual experiment. However, this is something that sociolinguists generally wouldn't want to do because it leads participants in a way that is undesirable given our research questions. Another possibility is to allow participants to listen to all of the tokens ahead of time and then to instruct them to use the entire scale. Of course, this is also not always desirable since the researcher may want to get the participant's first impression. A third option is to provide a clear description of the labels; while this does not anchor the points very solidly, this is generally the preferred route of sociolinguists.

What's that?

A **rating task** is a task in which participants indicate their response on a scale. There are many different kinds of rating tasks.

A **Likert scale** is a type of rating task in which the response involves agreement with some statement.

A **Visual Analog Scale (VAS)** is used for rating tasks in which the scale between the endpoints is continuous from the participants' point of view. While the data are not truly continuous, they are commonly analyzed as though they are.

In the **matched guise technique**, a single talker produces two versions of an utterance. The different versions of the utterance are known as **guises** and are used to set up the experimental conditions. The technique can be modified to use a single utterance that is manipulated using resynthesis to produce two versions.

In terms of the number of points on the scale, there is no right or wrong answer. You need enough points (> 3) to generate interesting results and to give the participants more options, and you don't want so many points (> 10) that distinctions between the points become meaningless to you or the participant.

You may have noticed that I'm using the term rating scale rather than Likert (pronounced with the short vowel /ɪ/) scale. The reason for this is that while all of these scales are sometimes referred to as Likert scales, some researchers reserve the use of this term to scales such as that in Example 3.1a that denote agreement since this is in line with how Rensis Likert himself used the scales (Likert 1932).

Some drawbacks of these sorts of rating scales are that the data are ordinal rather than continuous and that they limit participants to a predetermined set of responses and number of ticks. An alternative is to use a Visual Analog Scale (VAS) which provides anchors on each endpoint of a line but leaves it to participants to place a mark at any point on the line at the position they feel is most appropriate; there are no predetermined tickmarks along the scale. Llamas and Watt (2014) describe two types of VAS used in the Accent and Identity on the Scottish/English Border (AISEB) project. The first type used was an Attitudinal Analog Scale, for which participants responded to a statement such as that shown in Example 3.2a to show their level of agreement. The second was a Relational Analog Scale (shown in Example 3.2b) where participants were asked to select from a list of identity labels those they identified with, placing them in relative order and distance from one another based on how important they are to their identity. An advantage of a VAS over a rating task with tickmarks is that, from the viewpoint of the participant, they have a great deal of flexibility; a disadvantage is that only the endpoints can be anchored, which can make comparisons of responses across participants more difficult to interpret.

(3.2)

    a) "I feel British but I'm definitely more Scottish than anything else."
       Disagree_____ Agree

    b) Scottish   English   Borderer   European   Berwicker
       Least important_____ Most important

Watson and Clark (2015) extend the use of VAS even further, measuring changes in responses over time as the signal unfolds. While the use of VAS is still in its infancy in sociolinguistics, it has definite advantages over other types of rating scales, and it should be considered as an option by sociolinguists studying language attitudes.

In sociolinguistics, rating tasks often involve playing an auditory token and asking the participant to rate some characteristic using the scale provided. Auditory stimuli that are used for rating tasks vary. In most cases, creating the clips involves recording speakers and segmenting the recording into shorter clips that the listener responds to. The length of the clip varies across studies, with some researchers using long segments of speech, others using sentences, and still others using only a single word. Which one is right for you will depend on the extent to which you need multiple cues, including suprasegmental ones, in order to answer your research question. If using a single word, it's a good idea to inform participants of the identity of the word before they hear it in order to avoid potential ambiguity or to select words that are uniformly unambiguous for the listeners. For the latter, a norming study is necessary.

Commonly used with a rating task is the matched guise technique, which was developed by Lambert, Hodgson, Gardner, Fillenbaum (1960). In the matched guise technique, the same speaker is used to create stimuli for two (or more) conditions. The two versions produced by the speaker are called *guises*. The idea is that, because the speaker is the same, any differences will be minimized. For example, if I am running an experiment that looks at whether listeners identify speech from Region A as more pleasant sounding than speech from Region B and I do not use the same speaker for the two regions, the speakers I have chosen to record differ from one another in ways that are not necessarily representative of the regions themselves. For example, they might differ in how animated they are when reading the sentences, or they might have idiosyncratic speech characteristics, such as a particular voice quality. It is likely that listeners will judge some of the voices as less pleasant based on characteristics that have nothing to do with region. This would be detrimental for your study because it would affect the interpretation of the results. Thus, many researchers have opted to use the matched guise technique instead.

That said, it's not always possible or desirable to control the voices. The use of stimuli produced by different speakers across conditions is an appropriate method if investigating what might be considered global differences, such as dialects, language, or style, that critically differ in a wide range of linguistic cues. Further, bidialectal speakers may not be easy to find, and their realizations may differ from mono-dialectal speakers in the region in subtle ways that nonetheless may be socially meaningful for the listeners. Researchers who do not or cannot control the voice across experimental conditions should ensure that they have a large number of voices in each condition. In addition, a norming task should be used prior to running the experiment so that confounding factors can be balanced across conditions.

In the other extreme, there are research questions that require greater control than even the original matched guise technique can provide. A greater level of control can be achieved by using a modified version of the matched guise technique in which a single recording is modified using speech resynthesis. There is less control with unmodified voices because even repetitions of a single utterance produced by a single speaker will vary in the phonetic cues that are present in the signal. Thus, many researchers use a modified version of the matched guise technique in which a single production by a speaker is used, and the clip is digitally manipulated to create the two guises. This means that everything across guises is controlled except the specific linguistic cue(s) of interest. This method is most commonly used for phonetic, phonological, and morphological variants, but it could also be used to examine variation in perception due to lexical or syntactic variation.

While most researchers using modified speech to create guises have focused on a single linguistic variable, some researchers have looked at the interaction of multiple variables (Levon 2014) or at the effects of varying amounts of exposure to a variable (Labov, Ash, Ravindranath, Weldon, & Nagy 2011). Increasing the complexity of an experiment in these ways results in a greater number of complicating factors to consider when setting up the experiment. While such experiments can address interesting research questions, I advise you to start with a simpler experiment that focuses on a single variable, without varying amounts of exposure to that variable. Once you have the more basic experiment designed, run, and analyzed, then you can develop the design by adding layers to it. Below, I step through a sample experiment (Experiment 1). I begin with a simple experiment that uses digital manipulation for a modified version of the matched guise technique, with plans to add a layer to this experiment to create a follow-up experiment. Experiment 1 is designed to test whether listeners attribute different social characteristics to a speaker based on the presence or absence of discourse particle *like*. The follow-up experiment tests whether varying the frequency of discourse particle *like* influences the social characteristics attributed to a speaker.

This experiment will use a between-subjects design. I want to use 20 different voices for the target items (10 male and 10 female); listeners will hear all 20 target voices, but they will only hear one guise per talker. The target sentences are not identical but are on a similar topic to one another, and there is nothing in the semantic content that is socially salient. In addition to the target item, I am including 30 fillers in order to draw the attention away from the target items. This is necessary because I expect that, if attention is drawn toward discourse particle *like*, listeners will be more likely to indicate a difference between tokens with *like* and tokens without. However, attention is often not focused on *like* during normal interaction, so including the fillers can help to better approximate a more natural setting. The nature of the fillers needs to be carefully considered: using fillers without *like* might make the target tokens more salient than they would otherwise be due to their relative infrequency; using fillers with *like* might also make the target tokens more salient. Neither of these is desirable. For this experiment, I'm going to use fillers that do not contain the word *like* but instead contain something that is even more likely to attract the participant's attention, something that is completely unrelated to discourse pragmatic markers but that is something the participants are likely to (1) notice and (2) think that's what the experiment is about. Slang is one option that I would be worried about using here because I don't want to highlight word-level variation, particularly that which might be associated with youthfulness. Another option is including a non-standard syntactic or morpho-syntactic construction. If I go with this option, I want to focus on variation that is associated with social characteristics that discourse particle *like* is not stereotypically associated with. A third option would be to use talkers who have a variety of different non-native accents. This last one is the option I've chosen. I've done this for two reasons: (1) it provides an excellent distractor for the main purpose of the experiment, and (2) doing so allows me to build-in a pilot experiment for an unrelated study on the perceptions of different types of L2 accented speech.

To create the stimuli, I first recorded 30 native speakers of English who come from a single region. Each speaker was recorded reading all 40 target sentences, including some additional sentences in case any of the 20 are identified as weird or unnatural. They read each of the 20 target sentences multiple times: once without discourse particle *like*, once with it occurring once, and (because I might want it later for a follow-up experiment) once with it occurring twice or even three times. Care should be taken to vet the sentences for naturalness prior to recording (by getting ratings in a sentence naturalness task with real participants or, at the very least, by asking lab mates who are native speakers). In addition to these 30 voices, I record an additional 30 speakers, half of whom have L2 accented English, reading 40 sentences that are similar but not identical to the target sentences.

To create the guises, I use Praat to splice the token of *like* from the version of sentence 1 where it occurred, and I paste it into the version of sentence 1 that previously did not have *like*. Now I have two versions of sentence 1 that are identical except for the presence of the word *like*.

Before setting up the main experiment, I need to set up the naturalness task. This is necessary to determine which of the 30 voices I've recorded are the 20 voices I'll use in the experiment; whether the manipulation I conducted on the sentences is perceived as natural will determine which talkers I end up using. For the norming task, all of the participants hear all 30 voices producing both versions. Participants will rate the naturalness of the sentences. I then use these ratings to match naturalness scores across the different conditions.

Once the final 20 voices and target sentences have been identified, I am ready to set up and run my experiment. To set it up, I need to plan carefully regarding balancing (Section 2.1.6), randomization (Section 2.1.5), and repetition of stimuli (see Section 2.1.4). In this experiment, I am using 40 different target sentences, paired with male and female voices across four different lists, using a Latin Square so that each sentence is played once in each guise for both a male and a female voice. Each list contains only two sentences produced by the same speaker, and the two sentences appear in the opposite guise from one another. Each participant takes part in only one list in order to avoid repetition of the sentences. With four lists, I'm going to recruit around 32 participants with an aim of having 8 participants (4 men and 4 women) in each list.

I plan to use a VAS task to collect responses. I'm particularly interested in positive associations that listeners have with discursive *like*, so I will include questions such as those in Example 3.3.

(3.3)

"This person sounds like someone who I'd like to be friends with."
Disagree_____ Agree

"This person sounds like they hold or will one day hold a degree from an institute of higher learning."
Disagree_____ Agree

"I would trust this person to make good decisions based on common-sense."
Disagree_____ Agree

"This person sounds like someone who has an interest in fashion."
Disagree_____ Agree

For the analysis, I will convert responses to a linear scale and run a linear mixed effects model with speed of response as a control variable, participant and item as random intercepts, and by-item random slopes for guise (see Section 6.5.1).

All methods have drawbacks, including rating tasks. One drawback of rating tasks is that the experimenter cannot control how the listener interprets the stimuli and the questions: do different participants in a study have the same understanding of what 'cute' or 'Southern' or 'attractive' means? Because of this, there is likely to be a great deal of variation in responses. The best-designed studies use this to their advantage, anticipating and testing some of the factors that might correlate with the variation. Another drawback of rating tasks is that different participants may interpret the scale itself differently. This is especially problematic if any but not all datapoints from a subject are removed (due to, e.g., equipment error) because responses from a participant are only really meaningful within the context of that participants' other responses and, in a within subject design, within the context of that same participant's responses in the other condition. For example, imagine two different participants responding to a single question on a rating task that uses a scale from 1 to 5. Then say that the mean response of the first participant is 3.5 whereas the mean response of the second is 1.5 and, in response to Question #25, each of these participants provides a response of 3. For these two participants, a response of 3 indicates something very different. Because of this, a within-subjects design is much more interpretable for this type of task. However, many people continue to use a between-subjects design in an effort to disguise their research question.

One final drawback with this type of task is that it is not necessarily always measuring attitudes or opinions so much as it is capturing a willingness to report the attitudes and opinions. It is a meta-cognitive task, so participants are aware of what they are being asked even if they are not consciously aware of the specific hypothesis or do not notice the linguistic variation in the stimuli. Thus, when efforts aren't made to disguise the hypothesis, participants may be unwilling to report opinions that might make them look bad or they might report what they think the researcher wants them to say. This is not to say that the method shouldn't be used, but appropriate caution should be taken, both when designing the experiment and when interpreting the results, and triangulation should be used when possible.

Explore the methods

Materials from the following studies can be found on the companion website: https://www.bloomsbury.com/cw/experimental-research-methods-in-sociolinguistics/

matched guise

Purnell, Idsardi, and Baugh (1999)

Hilton and Gooskens (2013)

modified matched guise

Campbell-Kibler (2007, 2011)

Levon (2007, 2014)

Walker, García, Cortés, and Campbell-Kibler (2014)

modified matched guise with variation in the variable's frequency of occurrence

Levon and Buchstaller (2015)

Visual Analog Scale (VAS)

Llamas and Watt (2014)

open response task

Drager et al. (in prep)

3.1.2. Categorization task: social categories

What are some of the methods that can be used in addition to or instead of a rating task? Rather than asking participants to rate characteristics, some scholars have opted to ask participants to assign each talker to a category. For example, participants might be played a token (e.g., a talker saying *But it was still like three days away*) and then be asked to assign the speaker to a category (e.g., male vs. female; California vs. Wisconsin; North American vs. South African). Categorization tasks involving social categories are commonly used when investigating perceived region, helping researchers determine the accuracy of dialect identification or the association between particular variants or combinations of variants with a region. This type of task has also been used with children; when using this method with children, one should minimize the number of items that the children are being asked to categorize.

One benefit of this method is that, as long as there are only two possible categories presented at any given time, data from categorization tasks are relatively straightforward to analyze. Some critiques of this method are that it carries a heavier cognitive load than some other tasks (this is true of tasks involving metalinguistic decisions in general) and that some participants feel more comfortable working with a rating scale where they can choose a neutral option. In addition, some scholars have felt the data are too restrictive, resulting in a simplified understanding of the link between language and social meaning.

3.1.3. Open response

A less restrictive alternative to investigating person perception is the use of an open response format, playing auditory stimuli like those used in a rating task but holding focus groups or asking participants to write their open response answers to questions on an answer sheet. This technique is often used in tandem with a rating task or forced-choice task. In some cases, the results from an open response task are used to inform which rating or forced-choice questions will be used in subsequent experiments.

Prior to running the sample experiment discussed in Section 3.1.1, I might first like to run an experiment with the same auditory stimuli but with open response questions that help determine what anchors I should use in the VAS task. This can also help to develop a more nuanced understanding of what social characteristics are associated with discourse *like*. Thus, I could ask questions such as those in Example 3.4.

(3.4)

> How would you describe this person's style?
> How would you describe this person's personality?
> What are three words that you think probably best describe
> what this person looks like?
> (from Drager et al. in prep)

When running these types of tasks, it can be a good idea to give participants the chance to opt out from answering. It can also be a good idea to give them the opportunity to indicate how confident they are in their answer. Individuals differ in how comfortable they are answering such questions. It generally hasn't been a problem in studies I've been involved in, but – if you anticipate a participant population that is sensitive to such things – you may want to word the questions in ways that will make them feel comfortable, focusing, for example, on positive attributes.

Analyzing the data from an open response task is not as straightforward as analyzing data from a rating task. Most researchers treat the data qualitatively, selecting responses that are especially telling and informative, identifying words or phrases that have similar meanings as well as those that have opposite meanings. Tag clouds can be used to represent responses visually (see Drager & Kirtley 2016) or computational methods, such as Latent Dirichlet Allocation (LDA), can be used to explore relations between words used in the participants' responses (Schnoebelen & Drager 2014).

3.1.4. Implicit Association Tests

Implicit Association Tests (IAT) are used to explore attitudes that a participant has but that they are reluctant to divulge or that they might not even be aware of having. To examine attitudes, the IAT attempts to measure the strength of the associations between two concepts relative to the association between two other concepts. The task was initially designed to examine the degree to which participants associated different ethnicities (e.g., Black and White) with positive and negative traits. In the task, participants learn to associate one side of the screen with words or faces or sounds associated with a social category (e.g., one ethnic category) and the other side of the screen with a different but related social category (e.g., a different ethnic category). At the same time, they learn to associate positively or negatively valenced words with each of the sides. Then, the social categories are swapped. A sample slide based on work by Molly Babel is shown in Figure 3.1.

During the IAT, participants are asked to categorize different stimuli. The stimuli are designed to belong to one of two categories: the target category and the attribute category. For example, participants in Babel (2009) were asked to categorize the name Temeka (as shown in Figure 3.1) as well as categorize valenced words such as *paradise*. The target category can be a linguistic variable and the attribute category a social variable (Campbell-Kibler 2012) or, if data from the IAT are used to inform results from a different, linguistically related task, the target variable can be a social variable and the attribute variable a judgment of good or bad (Babel 2009). In most cases, the stimuli are presented as text, but they can also be presented auditorily (Campbell-Kibler 2012). Participants are instructed to ignore the target category when responding to an attribute stimulus and vice versa. The experiment has multiple blocks: Block 1 focuses only on training participants to categorize the target items (e.g., TEMEKA); Block 2 focuses only on the attribute items (e.g., *paradise*); Block 3 has both target and attribute items (as in Figure 3.1); Block 4 is just like Block 1 except the target categories are shown on opposite sides of the screen (e.g., the positions of BLACK and WHITE are reversed); Block 5 is like Block 3 except that the target categories are on the same sides of the screen as in Block 4 (e.g., pairing WHITE with *good*). More blocks can also be included (see Greenwald, McGhee, & Schwartz 1998, Greenwald et al. 2003), but I've used five here in line with Babel (2009, 2010). The researcher then compares the reaction times for the different pairings between the two social categories and the two categories of words. The idea is that, if the participant was faster at responding to a face when it was paired with the negatively valenced words, the participant is more biased than someone who is slower. However, as I discuss in Section 1.3.1, this interpretation should be viewed with a healthy level of skepticism.

Counterbalancing should be used when focusing on group attitudes rather than those of an individual. However, in most cases, sociolinguists have been interested in individual scores for each participant, comparing the scores for each participant relative to the other. In these cases, counterbalancing the position of the attributes across different groups of participants is undesirable; because which pairing a participant is exposed to first will influence their behavior in other blocks, counterbalancing the blocks introduces inter-subject differences that stem from the experiment design in addition to any differences between the subjects' implicit attitudes. Thus, when correlating individual IAT scores with scores on an explicit test, the two groups of participants should be tested separately if counterbalancing was used.

A similar task to the IAT is the Personalized Implicit Association Test (P-IAT). The P-IAT is like the IAT but is designed to focus on personal rather than extra-personal attitudes. For example, vegetables are associated widely with health, so an individual's extra-personal association

Figure 3.1   Screen during single trial for stimulus "Temeka" in Block 3 of the IAT. Based on Babel (2009)

is likely to be positive, but that individual might not like them, so their personal association would be negative. Methodologically, the only difference between IAT and P-IAT is that participants in the P-IAT categorize the associated concept in terms of *like-don't like* (see Rosseel, Speelman, & Geeraerts 2015), whereas participants in the IAT categorize according to some other categorization scheme (e.g., *good-bad*).

In both the IAT and the P-IAT, trials with response times longer than 10,000ms are removed prior to analysis. Following Greenwald, Nosek, and Banaji (2003), many scholars also opt to penalize incorrect responses by replacing the value for that item with the block mean + 600ms. However, in most research that uses reaction times, incorrect responses are removed from the analysis, and it is not clear that penalizing incorrect responses in the IAT is in fact the most appropriate method. Therefore, I advise caution with using this approach until the implications of this choice have been explored by researchers who are unaffiliated with the original developers of the IAT. Participant scores are then calculated as the difference between the means of the test blocks (Block 5–Block 3). Greenwald et al. (2003) then suggest dividing this by the standard deviation of the test blocks.

What's the difference?

An **Implicit Association Test (IAT)** is a sorting task in which response times are measured. In the task, participants are asked to sort emotionally valenced items into categories and to sort socially indexed names, concepts, or items into socially associated categories.

A **Personalized Implicit Association Test (P-IAT)** is identical to the IAT except the categories are *like-don't like* instead of *good-bad*.

The **Social Category Association Test (SCAT)** is like an IAT except there are no correct responses.

3.1.5. The Social Category Association Test

Like the IAT, the Social Category Association Test (SCAT) compares response times over multiple blocks (see Llamas, Watt, & MacFarlane 2016 discussed in Section 1.3.1). However, there are no correct answers with SCAT. Instead, participants are asked to match a stimulus (e.g., an auditory token containing a particular vowel realization) with one of two categories, where the matching is based entirely on the participants' opinion. The speed of responding is interpreted as a measure of the strength of the association between the category and the item being categorized. An example slide is shown in Figure 3.2.

If comparing differences in words, it is important to run a norming experiment (using e.g., a lexical decision task) because not all words are processed with equal speed. If comparing differences in phonetic realizations, words potentially made ambiguous by the variation (e.g., *cheater* and *cheetah* for some talkers of a non-rhotic variety) should be avoided.

Explore the methods

Materials from the following studies are available on the companion site website: https://www.bloomsbury.com/cw/experimental-research-methods-in-sociolinguistics/

Implicit Association Test

Babel (2009)

Social Category Association Test

Llamas et al. (2016)

Figure 3.2 Screen during single trial for stimulus [kɑɹ] (a rhotic realization of *car*) in the SCAT. Based on Llamas et al. (2016)

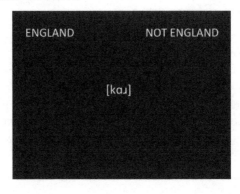

3.2. Social factors influencing perception

3.2.1. Phoneme monitoring task

A method that can be used to examine the perception of sounds is **phoneme monitoring**. In a phoneme monitoring task, listeners hear auditory stimuli and are asked to indicate whether the stimulus contains the target sound or not. Phoneme monitoring can be used to address sociolinguistic questions, especially those surrounding markedness or salience, or those that aim to compare perception across two participant populations that differ in some social domain, such as region of origin. In the sample experiment below, I use real words, but other versions of this task type involve covering the target sound with noise and using pseudowords.

To demonstrate, I use as an example an experiment (which, to my knowledge, has never been conducted) that investigates the extent to which participants are more likely to perceive a regional variant when it is stereotypically associated with a talker's region of origin. During the experiment, Spanish speakers will be asked to listen for the sound [j]. The glide is a variant of /ʎ/ (as in *calle* 'street') in many Latin American varieties whereas [ʎ] is retained in most parts of Bolivia (see overview in Lipski 2011). In Argentine Spanish, /ʎ/ is realized as [ʒ] or, increasingly, [ʃ] (Chang 2008). Using this method, we can explore the extent to which participants from three regions – Bolivia (where it is realized as [ʎ]), Guatemala (where it is realized as [j]), and Argentina (where it is realized as [ʃ]) – notice the sound [j] when the talker is from the same dialect as them compared to when the talker comes from a different dialect region. In addition, we can run a follow-up experiment to explore whether priming a dialect area makes it more likely that participants will respond that they heard [j], even when the acoustic signal does not contain [j] but contains [ʃ] or has been covered in noise.

To set up the task, I first need to identify target words where [j] is a variant. I also need to come up with fillers: some that contain /j/ phonemically (e.g., *playa* 'beach') and others where the target sound is not possible as a variant (e.g., *perro* 'dog'). Then, I will record three speakers, one from each region. The speakers should be as similar as possible to one another in terms of social characteristics other than their regional background. The speakers will produce each target word twice, once with [ʃ] and once with an alternative realization.

In the first version of the experiment, I will block by region in order to increase the likelihood that listeners will use their expectations about the dialect during the task. If results from the first experiment indicate that listeners use their expectations about the speaker during the phoneme monitoring task, I will then conduct a follow-up experiment (with a different set of participants) in which tokens are not blocked by speaker.

If using a phoneme monitoring task, it is critical that some training session be used. This is especially important for this type of task since it's unnatural and participants may be inclined to rely on spelling even though the words are not written. During the training session, only words where /j/ is phonemic should be played, and they should be different items than the fillers. Also included should be tokens where the phoneme is /j/ but the realization is not (e.g., speakers from northern Mexico realizing /j/ as [ʃ]). This way, participants can be trained to focus on pronunciation rather than on spelling. In some cases, it may also be necessary to play tokens that contain the target sound as a variant of a different phoneme. (See, e.g., the practice task used by Hay, Drager, & Gibson forthcoming, available on the companion website.)

The strengths of this paradigm are that it allows researchers to examine the perception of sounds in contexts where minimal pairs are rare or non-existent. The drawbacks are that it focuses attention on the target phoneme, which is undesirable for some research questions.

Explore the methods

Materials from the following experiments are available on the companion website: https://www.bloomsbury.com/cw/experimental-research-methods-in-sociolinguistics/

phoneme monitoring

Hay et al. (forthcoming)

identification task

Hay, Warren, and Drager (2006b)

Squires (2013a)

discrimination tasks

AX: Experiment 3 from Girard, Floccia, and Jeremy Goslin (2008)

AXB: Riverin-Coutlée and Arnaud (2015)

matching task

Niedzielski (1999)

transcription task

McGowan (2015)

sentence plausibility task

Hilton, Haug, and Gooskens (2013)

lexical decision task

Kim (2016)

Llompart and Simonet (forthcoming)

3.2.2. Identification task

In **an identification task**, listeners hear a sound, word, or series of words, and they are asked to identify what they heard. Identifying what they heard usually involves selecting which of the provided options most closely matches what was perceived. Open response answers are also possible and, when used, are referred to as **word recognition tasks** or **commutation tasks**. They're attractive because the task more closely approximates speech perception in the wild, but they involve more work and "fuzzy" decision-making when coding the data since decisions about whether or not a response was correct are not always clear-cut. In addition, nonsensical responses need to be discarded.

Regardless of whether or not forced-choice responses are used, identification tasks are one my personal favorite types of tasks because they are relatively easy to set up and can be used to collect both responses and reaction times. They can also be used for a large number of different research questions, including testing intelligibility (Section 1.3.2), whether social primes affect perception (Section 1.3.3), and whether sounds are merged in perception (Section 1.5). Noise is often overlaid onto the recordings since this leads to more variation in responses and reaction times, but this is not necessary in cases when confusability is anticipated to be especially high. While the auditory stimuli are most frequently produced by speakers unfamiliar to the participant, some scholars have used tokens produced by the participants or by people known to the participants (e.g., Labov, Yaeger, & Steiner 1972).

Despite their many virtues, identification tasks aren't appropriate for everything. For starters, the task is less natural than some other options and a large number of fillers are normally necessary. (See Section 2.1.3 for more on fillers.)

One thing to consider when designing an identification task is whether the response screen should contain written text (as in Figure 3.3a) or images (Figure 3.3b). Since many words are not easily visualized as images, using written words means that a larger number of unique words can be used. Written words are common in perception tasks in sociolinguistic work on perception, despite definite advantages to using images instead (see Section 2.1.1). We know so little about the timing of accessing social information compared with the timing of accessing other kinds of information, that some of these questions really need to be explored before we can know the full impact of some of our past methodological decisions.

When identifying words to be used on the task, token frequency and the real word status of the item both make a difference. Identification is

Figure 3.3   Example response screen for a binary forced-choice task, using (a) written text, as shown in the left panel, and (b) images, as shown in the right panel

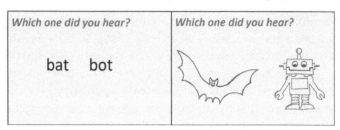

biased toward real words and more frequent words. The larger the number of individual items used in the experiment, the more difficult it is to control token frequency, in which case token frequency should be balanced across conditions.

As an example, here I provide a subset of tokens from an experiment investigating what factors influence perception of TRAP, which is backing into the space of LOT in this dialect (e.g., California English). A six-step continuum between the vowels is created for each of the target items, with smaller numbered tokens indicating a fronter vowel (rVck1 is unambiguously *rack* and rVck6 is unambiguously *rock*). The filler items are intended to distract participants' attention away from variation in the vowels since they are minimal pairs or near-minimal pairs that differ in the initial phoneme, or they are homonyms for the speaker (e.g., *which-witch*) that differ only in spelling. None of the filler items contains either of the target vowels. The experiment is blocked by initial consonant, and this is a portion of the block that involves /w/ and /r/, so it contains the target items, *rock-rack*, *rot-rat*, and *wok-whack*, and the filler items, *whim-rim*, *woo-roo* and *while-rile*, as shown in Figure 3.4. Other blocks use other phonological environments and target items (e.g., *bot-bat*). The order is pseudorandomized so that target items occur at irregular intervals.

The analysis will compare the cross-over points (i.e., when along the continuum participants switch from hearing *rack* to hearing *rock*) across whatever conditions are being tested (e.g., experiment instructions read by a speaker from Minnesota – where speakers produce raised variants of the TRAP vowel – or a speaker from California who produces retracted variants of TRAP.)

When setting up the experiment, be sure to remember that, ideally, everything should be balanced that is not controlled (see Sections 1.1 and 2.1.1). This includes the order of the responses on the screen, the order of the blocks, and characteristics of the participants across conditions.

Figure 3.4   Stimuli for the /r/-/w/ block from the example identification task, where target items are shown with an ambiguous vowel (V) and a number representing a point in the vowel continuum

order	auditory token	word-pair	token type
1	whim	whim-rim	filler
2	roo	woo-roo	filler
3	rule	wool-rule	filler
4	rVck3	rock-rack	target
5	rim	whim-rim	filler
6	wVck2	wok-whack	target
7	wick	wick-Rick	filler
8	rule	wool-rule	filler
9	rile	while-rile	filler
10	rVt5	rot-rat	target
11	white	white-right	filler
12	rick	wick-Rick	filler
13	wVck6	wok-whack	target
14	woo	woo-roo	filler
15	which	which-witch	filler
16	whim	whim-rim	filler
17	rile	while-rile	filler
18	witch	which-witch	filler
19	rVt3	rot-rat	target
20	rick	wick-Rick	filler
21	rVck2	rock-rack	target
22	white	white-right	filler
23	rim	whim-rim	filler
24	wVck4	wok-whack	target
25	while	while-rile	filler
26	right	white-right	filler
27	wool	wool-rule	filler
28	woo	woo-roo	filler
29	rVck5	rock-rack	target
30	which	which-witch	filler
31	right	white-right	filler
32	rVt1	rot-rat	target

When synthesizing a continuum for these purposes, I normally begin by synthesizing the entire continuum but then I conduct pilot work to determine where the perceptual boundary is likely to fall. Ideally, the boundary spans several steps of the continuum; without this, participants are likely to get a ceiling effect. Since the effect of social information on phone perception is subtle, variability in responses (i.e., ambiguity) is likely essential in order to observe an effect at all. (This is my best guess as to why Chang (2015) reports no effect of regional label in his experiment on the perception of a retroflex-alveolar distinction in Mandarin. There appears to be an effect in his data, but only for one of the vowel contexts and only when responses are not at ceiling.)

Work focusing on phonetic and phonological properties has long dominated sociolinguistic experimental work. There are, however, a number of interesting and timely questions to explore at other levels of the grammar, and identification tasks are an appropriate method for looking at how listeners interpret syntactic variation or a sentence rendered ambiguous in its structure. Using this paradigm, a sentence is played and then participants can select which of the choices provided (as a picture or written text) is consistent with how they interpreted the sentence. In some cases (see Squires 2013a), white noise can be used to mask the target word(s), so that listeners must rely on other cues in the signal to determine the intended word.

Regardless of which level of the grammar is the focus, priming of different sorts can be used, and this is where this paradigm gets especially interesting for sociolinguists. Primes can be made up of text (e.g., a standard vs. non-standard sentence structure), auditory stimuli (e.g., to incorporate prosodic cues or voice quality), or visual stimuli (e.g., faces of people with social characteristics associated with the different structures). Likewise, primes can interact with other factors of interest. For example, priming with non-standard sentence structures could hypothetically increase the number of interpretations that are consistent with the non-standard structure if played in the same voice as the prime but not in a novel voice.

3.2.3. Discrimination task

Discrimination tasks are similar to identification tasks and can be used to explore similar questions, but they are most often used to examine the perception of sounds that are undergoing a merger or for which there is a 2-1 correspondence across languages. Alternatively, they can be used to test whether listeners can discriminate between talkers or varieties (see e.g., Girard et al. 2008). In a discrimination task, the stimulus is made up of two (or more) words, and participants are asked to identify whether they are pronounced the same or differently. Normally, the words are played in isolation, but contexts could also be used as long as they don't disambiguate the word. Unlike in an identification task, participants do not normally see the words written if the task is about perception. Discrimination tasks can also be run as production tasks or as tasks that require more introspection (see e.g., the odd one out task in Section 4.2.4). When responding to a target item in a discrimination task that involves perception of a merger, unmerged listeners should respond that the words are different. However, it's important to include other items, too. Some distractors should contain the target sounds but for which the correct answer is "same" (e.g., *pier* and *peer*), so that the researcher can remove (or given special consideration to) participants who respond that these tokens are "different" (a possible response for participants from New Zealand who have a vowel merger with *pear* and *pier/peer* but believe they maintain a distinction). Alternatively, these items could be tested as a different set of target items. If this is done, they should be analyzed separately from the other kinds of target items. It is also a good idea to include a set of fillers that is easily distinguishable as different (e.g., *pig* and *big* produced by L1 speakers of English) and another that is easily distinguishable as the same (e.g., *pier* and *peer* in American English). These items should be selected on the basis of some other characteristic that will distract participants' attention away from the target variable.

As an example, I now step through a discrimination task designed to examine the perception of stop consonants in Korean. Korean famously has a three-way contrast for voiceless stops: aspirated, lenis, and fortis. Traditionally, distinctions between realizations are maintained through voice onset time (VOT) – the duration between the burst and the start of voicing – where aspirated stops have the longest VOT and fortis stops the shortest. However, many young speakers of Seoul Korean no longer use VOT to differentiate their productions of aspirated and lenis stops, instead relying on f0 in the following vowel to signal the contrast and female speakers seem to be leading the change (Kim 2014). In the sample experiment, we are concerned with (1) do listeners shift in whether they use VOT or f0 to identify the plosive and (2) what factors influence the shift? We hypothesize that the gender of the listener and the gender attributed to the talker will influence perception. Specifically, we predict that pairs that differ in VOT but not f0 will be more likely to be identified as "different" by male listeners, and by female listeners if the token is perceived as having been produced by a man. The test stimuli are tokens produced by two speakers (one male and one female), and the speech is manipulated to create four talkers, two of whom are likely to be perceived as male and two of whom are likely to be perceived as female. This is achieved by lowering the formants (including f0) of the original female speaker and raising the formants (including f0) of the original male speaker. A VOT continuum with traditional aspirated and fortis stops as endpoints is created. The stimuli are blocked by voice. By blocking by voice, the social information attributed to the talker is likely to have a stronger effect than if voices varied within block; subsequent experiments should vary the talker within the block in order to verify any effects observed in the sample experiment.

An already-existing example of a binary, forced-choice discrimination task is the third experiment reported in Girard et al. (2008). In their experiment, children (who were exposed to the task as a game) listened to sentences (e.g., *La soupe de ma grand-mère est bien meilleure quand elle rajoute une carotte;* 'My grandmother's soup is much tastier when she adds a carrot') that were produced by talkers from two different regions, identifying them as either the same or different. Materials from Girard et al. (2008) are available on the companion website.

3.2.4. AXB task

An AXB task is a type of perceptual discrimination task in which participants hear a series of three auditory stimuli. Two of the stimuli (A and B) are similar but differ in some regard, and participants are asked to compare A and B to a third stimulus (X). For example, I might be interested in L2 speakers' ability to perceive differences in place of articulation, so the place of articulation differs between A and B while everything else (e.g., manner of articulation and talker identity) remain constant. Then, the participant compares these to token X, which would have the same place of articulation as either A or B but is not an identical token. In fact, it is often a good idea for token X to have been produced by a different talker than A or B. The AXB task has several iterations (e.g., AXB, ABX, XAB) that differ depending on the placement of the token that listeners are asked to disambiguate. An example of a study that uses an AXB discrimination task is Riverin-Coutlée and Arnaud (2015), which compares perception of sounds across listeners from two different regions in Quebec. An example from their experiment is shown in Example 3.3, and further materials from the study can be found on the companion website.

(3.3)

> A: bai[ɛ]s   X: baie[ɛ]s   B: bai[ɛ]s
> (based on *baies* 'berries' example from Riverin-Coutlée and Arnaud (2015); A, X, and B are three talkers of the same sex)

The task can be used to look at perception, but it can also be a way to quantify shifts in production, especially those that arise from speaker accommodation. To use it this way, A and B are tokens of the same word recorded at different points in time (e.g., once before interacting with an interlocutor and once after) and token X is the same word produced by the interlocutor. A group of listeners then identifies whether A or B sounds more like X, which can help the researcher determine whether (perceptually) there has been convergence or divergence. In some cases, researchers have used spontaneously produced words recorded at the beginning of an inter-action (A) versus a word recorded at the end of the same interaction (B). This has the advantage of using spontaneous speech but means that the words will vary, making it more difficult to interpret what the results really mean.

The advantages of this type of task are that researchers can identify just noticeable differences, as well as which differences fall below the "just noticeable" threshold. The disadvantages are that the task requires hold-ing sounds in memory, which can influence responses. Thus, it is critical that the stimuli are counterbalanced appropriately and, when addressing certain kinds of questions, it can be a good idea to combine an AXB task with other kinds of tasks. Likewise, it should not be used to elicit response times.

3.2.5. Matching task

In a **matching task**, participants listen to a word or a phrase and they match some part of it (e.g., an underlined word) to a second set of stim-uli. An illustration is shown in Example 3.4, where numbers on the answersheet correspond with tokens from an auditory continuum. This is the approach used by Niedzielski (1999) in her study on the effect of a listener's expectations about the talker on the perception of sounds, and which Jen Hay and I used to explore similar questions in New Zealand (Hay, Nolan, & Drager 2006a, Hay & Drager 2010). The second set of stimuli used in this implementation of the design is a series of tokens that, together, make up a continuum between sounds.

(3.4) auditory token: "*During the colder months John and I both wanted to stay fit.*"

answer sheet: During the colder months John and I both wanted to stay fit.

1   2   3   4   5   6

(from Hay & Drager 2010)

The stimuli used by Niedzielski (1999) are available on the companion website.

A matching task is in many ways like an AXB task because it involves holding sounds in memory before responding, but it may be even more susceptible because the delay is often greater due to the larger number of tokens being played. Therefore, it would be a good idea for any studies that use this method to be revisited using other techniques.

3.2.6. Coach test

One disadvantage of the tests described above is that they focus the listener's attention on the variable. In addition, while filler items can help to lessen the degree of attention, the task is still artificial; hearing words in isolation and out of context is not how we normally encounter them, and this influences how we perceive them. One clever way to address these concerns is through using a **coach test** (Labov 2001: 403–406). In a coach test, participants hear a short narrative in which there is a word that is made ambiguous by the target variable for some listeners and which the context does not disambiguate (see Example 3.5). After hearing the story, participants are asked questions about what happened, and their answers to the questions reveal how they interpreted the ambiguous word. They are asked to listen to the ambiguous portion of the clip again but, this time, the clip is played in the opposite guise. Participants without a vowel merger in this word will most often switch their interpretation of the sentence, assuming they misheard it the first time.

(3.5)

    a) I gotta play Merion there.
    b) I gotta play Murray in there.
       (from Labov 2001)

While an exceptionally clever way to address the disadvantages of identification and discrimination tasks, coach tests also have drawbacks. The biggest of these is the small number of responses that can be elicited from a single participant due to the relatively large amount of time it takes to complete. This means that a coach test is not appropriate to answer certain questions (e.g., the effect of social information on perception) and that it is best combined in tandem with other methods of elicitation.

3.2.7. Transcription tasks

Transcription tasks are an excellent way to obtain perception data without imposing research-held expectations about what the listener will hear.

In these tasks, participants listen to clips of speech and are asked to transcribe what they hear. The experiment design should follow all of the "rules" laid out in Chapter 2, including controlling (or balancing) the number of words and syllables in each stimulus, and balancing expected answers if specific variables are being tested.

The example comes from McGowan (2015), in which participants heard high- and low-predictability English sentences produced by a native speaker of Mandarin Chinese. Tokens were covered in noise (i.e., multi-talker babble), making them more difficult to understand. An example of a low-predictability sentence from his experiment is shown in Example 3.6. The full set of auditory stimuli is available for download from the companion website.

(3.6)

> Dad pointed at the grass.
> (from McGowan 2015)

Upon hearing a token such as that in Example 3.6, participants were asked to write down, as carefully as possible, what was said.

Now comes the tricky part: coding the data as correct or not. Coding data from this type of task is tricky because it's not always clear what should be considered a correct answer (e.g., would <gass> be a misspelling of *grass* (which could be coded as correct) or *gas* (which would be coded as incorrect)?). Nor is it always clear which aspects of the utterance should be analyzed; for example, McGowan could have coded whether the entire sentence was correct (in which case <Dad pointed to the grass> would be incorrect), but he instead coded accuracy based only the last word in the sentence. This was probably the right decision – it is simpler and requires fewer researcher judgments – but the alternative might be more appropriate for other research questions, especially those focused on levels of the grammar higher than the phoneme. For experiments that involve transcription of multi-word utterances, responses can be coded as number of words incorrect or, alternatively, responses with any single word mistranscribed could be coded as incorrect.

3.2.8. Translation tasks: intelligibility

When investigating intelligibility, one alternative to using a transcription task is to use a **translation task**. During these tasks, participants listen to utterances, though the exact nature of the task varies. In some cases, participants are simply asked to translate the utterances into another language, usually by writing down what was said. In such tasks, the stimuli are set up the same way as in transcription tasks, but participants are asked to translate the sentences instead of transcribing them. Likewise, the design is highly similar to the translation tasks used to study production (Section 4.1.3). One difference is that those that test for intelligibility almost exclusively rely on auditory stimuli for spoken languages. Coding this type of translation task involves many of the difficult there's-no-good-answer decisions required during a transcription task. For example, it is not always easy to distinguish between whether a participant failed to provide all details from the original utterance due to a lack of understanding or if they were simplifying the task by only responding to those items or topics that they deemed the most relevant. Thus, care should be taken during the design of the translation task to simplify the coding process. For example, one might want to consider using a different type of translation task, such as one that involves listening to words or utterances from one language and selecting forced-choice responses in another.

3.2.9. Sentence verification and plausibility test

Another type of task used to investigate intelligibility is a sentence verification or plausibility test. For these, participants listen to utterances and are asked to judge whether the sentence is true or not (sentence verification) or whether it is plausible or not (sentence plausibility). The latter was used by Hilton et al. (2013) to test the extent to which Danish listeners understood Norwegian sentence structures. Examples of plausible and implausible sentences are provided in Example 3.7 and the full set of auditory stimuli can be downloaded from the companion website.

(3.7)

     plausible: Februar er den korteste måneden
     'February is the shortest month'
     implausible: Du lukter med hendene dine
     'You smell with your hands'
     (from Hilton et al. 2013)

Analyses of data from sentence verification and plausibility tests are straightforward because they are forced-choice tasks. In addition, in a plausibility test, both plausible and implausible sentences are used as stimuli, so the task does not lead participants to the correct response despite its forced-choice design. The task is an appropriate way to test intelligibility in cases when intelligibility is hypothesized to be fairly high because it requires comprehension of multiple words from each utterance.

3.2.10. Gating tasks

In experimental work, gating is when a target sound, word, or words are played to listeners and, with each iteration (i.e., gate), a greater amount of context for the token is provided. In these tasks, participants are asked to listen to the stimuli and respond, usually as an open response, with what they heard. They can also be asked to rate their confidence in the response they gave. The targets are most often played in isolation the first time they are played. An example is shown in Example 3.8, where they first respond after hearing a word in isolation (Example 3.8a), then a phrase, and then a sentence.

(3.8)

a) "[blæːk]"
   What was said? _____
   How confident are you that this was indeed what the speaker said?
   1 2 3 4 5 6 7
b) "living on one [blæːk]"
   What was said?   living on one _____
   How confident are you that this was indeed what the speaker said?
   1 2 3 4 5 6 7
c. "senior citizens living on one [blæːk]"
   What was said?   Senior citizens _____.
   How confident are you that this was indeed what the speaker said?
   1 2 3 4 5 6 7

(based on Labov (2010: 60–62), with a confidence rating task added)

In Labov's experiments, the iterations of target words occur across separate tasks, so that participants respond to all target words before passing through the next gate.

3.2.11. Lexical decision task

In **lexical decision tasks**, the researcher measures how long it takes for a participant to identify a stimulus as a real word in order to gain insight into what factors hinder or help the processing of words. Lexical decision tasks are commonly used by psycholinguists, but they are underused in sociolinguistics, probably due to the fact that they require a more complicated design and more experimental know-how than some other methods. However, I encourage sociolinguists to adopt this method, especially those who already have some experimental training and who wish to expand their methodological repertoire.

When might I use a lexical decision task? Let's say I'm interested in running an experiment investigating whether words associated with the American South (e.g., *grits*) are comprehended more quickly when they are heard in a Southern US accent than when they are produced by someone from, say, California. With a task like this, I don't anticipate there will be much variation in their responses (i.e., real word or non-word), but I hypothesize that listeners will be slower to respond to the Southern words when they are produced by someone who is not from the South.

The first step to setting up this experiment is to find appropriate lexical items. I plan to use four sets of words: (1) one set of Southern (real) words, (2) one set of real words that are region-neutral, (3) one set of real word distractors (see Section 2.1.3), and (4) and one set of pseudowords. The real words in (1) are the critical items and those in (2) make up the controls; I plan to analyze responses to all of these items. To identify appropriate words for these sets, I can mine a corpus (see Section 4.1.1) or, if I'm interested in stereotypical words, I can try to come up with words on my own. Across the sets, the words should be controlled for linguistic factors (e.g., number of syllables) or balanced for factors that cannot be controlled within the confines of the word requirements (e.g., token frequency and phonotactic probability). I then need to conduct a norming task to make sure that the words are perceived as either "Southern" or "region neutral." I also need to conduct a task to determine that the voices I plan to use are controlled in terms of any social factors that might also be perceived as related to some of the lexical items (e.g., ethnicity).

The design of the example experiment described above is similar to that employed by Kim (2016), who found that a talker's age would influence the perception of Korean words associated with people of a similar age. To test this, he used a lexical decision task, where participants heard words (such as those in Example 3.9) produced by talkers of different ages.

(3.9)

>young-associated word:
>꽈잠바   kkwacampa
>"a jacket worn by students in a department to mark their sense of solidarity"

old-associated word:
안사돈   ansaton
"one's daughter-in-law's [or son-in-law's] mother"

A full list of the words used for Kim (2016) is available at http://dx.doi. org/10.5334/labphon.33.s1, and the auditory stimuli and E-Prime scripts are downloadable from the companion website for this text.

Luckily, scholars in other fields have developed and made available lists of words with a number of word-related factors (e.g., average reaction times to the words) already calculated. See, for example, the English Lexicon Project (Balota et al. 2007) which is available online at http:// elexicon.wustl.edu. While extremely valuable, such resources rarely include all of the social information that sociolinguists might need to consider, so additional norming is often necessary.

One alternative to a lexical decision task is a **semantic decision task**, where participants are asked to identify information about a word's semantics. For example, the task might be to identify whether a lexical item refers to an animate object or not (see e.g., Adank & McQueen 2007). In such tasks, reaction times are analyzed in addition to accuracy.

3.3. Chapter Summary

Perception experiments offer a wide range of possibilities for exploring sociolinguistic research questions, ranging from those that focus on perception of the talker to those that focus more on perception of speech.

Take-home points

- There are many different kinds of perception tasks to choose from.
- Start simple and then build on the original experiment.
- Start by deciding your research question and then select the most appropriate method to answer the question.
- Based on pilot data, decide how you will code and analyze the data prior to data collection.
- If you want to avoid having to make tough decisions during data analysis, you may need to adjust your design prior to running the experiment.

Further reading

Clopper, Cynthia (2013). Experiments. In Christine Mallinson, Becky Childs, and Gerard Van Herk (Eds.) *Data Collection in Sociolinguistics: Methods and applications*. New York/London: Routledge, 151–161.

Clopper, Cynthia G., Jennifer Hay, and Bartlomiej Plichta (2011). Experimental speech perception and perceptual dialectology. In Marianna Di Paolo and Malcah Yaeger-Dror (Eds.) *Sociophonetics: A student's guide*. New York: Routledge, 149–162.

Drager, Katie (2013). Experimental methods in sociolinguistics. In Janet Holmes and Kirk Hazen (Eds.) *Research Methods in Sociolinguistics: A practical guide*. Oxford: Wiley-Blackwell, 58–73.

McGuire, Grant (2010). A brief primer on experimental designs for speech perception research. Unpublished manuscript, available from https://people.ucsc.edu/~gmcguir1/experiment_designs.pdf.

Prieto, Pilar (2012). Experimental methods and paradigms for prosodic analysis. In Abigail C. Cohn, Cécile Fougerson, and Marie K. Huffman (Eds.) *The Oxford Handbook of Laboratory Phonology*. Oxford: Oxford University Press, 528–538.

Thomas, Erik R. (2002). Sociophonetic applications of speech perception experiments. *American Speech* 77(2): 115–147.

Thomas, Erik R. (2011). *Sociophonetics: An introduction*. Basingstoke: Palgrave Macmillan.

Experimental designs to examine production

4

A primary strength of production experiments is their efficiency.

– Cynthia Clopper (2013: 151)

Sociolinguists use many different methods that focus on the production of speech, so what are some advantages of the methods that are experimental? Without a doubt, the advantages are efficiency and control. By controlling factors that are not the primary focus of the study, the researcher can achieve a higher level of certainty in the results and elicit large numbers of the target variable. Thus, experimenters can design experiments to examine linguistic variables that are infrequent in naturally occurring conversations and, with a greater amount of control, they can be more certain that any results are not due to extraneous factors.

Some of the methods described in this chapter are not strictly experimental in and of themselves, but they can be useful as tasks to add on to a larger experiment, or a manipulation could be added, making them experimental. For example, some possible manipulations include using a confederate as an interlocutor who varies their speech or behavior across conditions, priming with objects on the screen or in the room, overtly telling participants information that is intended to influence their mood, or using experimenters who come from different dialect regions. When following the experimental method, a high level of control is necessary. In Section 4.1, I discuss methods that can be used to address a variety of different research questions. In Section 4.2, I discuss surveys and questionnaires, including both those used to collect speech data as well as those used to explore more introspective questions about, for example, language use or language ideologies. An example experiment with tasks from Sections 4.1 and 4.2 is presented in Section 4.3. In Section 4.4, I focus on methods that are particularly well suited to investigate speech accommodation. A second example production experiment, one incorporating several tasks from Section 4.4, is described in Section 4.5.

4.1. Multi-purpose tasks

4.1.1. Interviews, conversations, and corpora

Sociolinguists love conversational data, and for good reason. It's rich in variation, and variation at all levels of the grammar can be studied. Labov (1966) set the standard for conducting interviews as a way of obtaining spoken language data. This involves controlling the order of topics and asking questions (such as the "Danger of Death" question) that invoke an emotional narrative. A large number of scholars have used and continue to use this method – or adaptations of this method – to explore sociolinguistic variation.

In an effort to further decrease influence from the researcher, some scholars ask participants to self-record at home or in other natural settings (see e.g., Podesva 2007; Sharma 2011; Kirtley 2015). Comparing results from interview data and self-recorded data, Sharma (2011) demonstrates how results based solely on interview data can be misleading, and there is preliminary evidence that self-recording leads to higher rates of innovative variants than interviews conducted by an experimenter (Boyd, Elliot, Fruehwald, Hall-Lew, & Lawrence 2015). While there are clear advantages to self-recording, this method also provides less control than an interviewer-led conversation, so its appropriateness depends on the extent to which the elicitation of innovative variants is more desirable than a higher level of control over influencing factors given the research question. Another option is to record dyads discussing a provided topic (e.g., Szakay 2012, where the topic was rugby and other sports); this controls for topic and may approximate a non-research setting, assuming that the topic of conversation is natural for all participants. The most enlightening sociolinguistic studies are likely to be those that use a range of methods, from those that prioritize naturalness to those with a high level of control.

Conversations can serve as the primary data from an experiment. In order to test a specific hypothesis, the researcher can introduce a trigger in different conditions and then compare behavior in the conditions to test whether that trigger had an effect. This is often done across subjects, but a within-subject approach can also be used. For example, Rickford and McNair-Knox (1994) manipulated the identity of the interviewer in examining whether speakers produce different linguistic variants depending on their interlocutor's ethnicity.

For conversational data using the experimental method, the researcher must carefully consider the conditions, controlling as much as possible the topics discussed (unless, of course, topic is the factor of interest that varies across condition). The same experimenter/interviewer should be used for all participants (unless, again, that is the factor being manipulated). Other than that, there is very little that can be controlled without making the conversation seem, well, less conversational. However, note that the rules of balancing and counterbalancing discussed in Chapter 2 apply. This means that – if manipulating experimenter identity and every participant meets with both experimenters – the number of participants who meet with Experimenter A prior to meeting with Experimenter B should equal the number who meet with Experimenter B first. And if topic can't be controlled (e.g., if, due to a within-subject design, repeating topics across different experimenters would lead to undesirable consequences), the topic should be counterbalanced across the different orders of experimenters.

When analyzing linguistic variables, the rules for controlling and balancing laid out in Section 2.1.1 apply. This method follows that pioneered by William Labov. As an example, a sample of fake data from a variationist study investigating form variation among quotatives (e.g., *She* said *"blah"* vs. *She* was like *"blah"*) is shown in Figure 4.1. Here

Figure 4.1   Example of data from a fake study on quotatives

	A	B	C	D	E	F	G
1	pseudonym	quotative	full.quote	quote.content	time.tense	person	mimetic
2	DrDre	be.like	She was like "I need chocolate"	reported.speech	past	third	y
3	DrDre	tell	He told me "you should sit down for this"	reported.speech	past	third	n
4	DrDre	be.like	so then I'm like "it all turned out ok"	thought	HP	first	n

you can see the example sentence, quotative verbs, and several linguistic and social factors hypothesized to correlate with which quotative is produced. The analysis will compare the number of times one of the variants (e.g., *be like*) is used to the number of times it could have been used but another quotative (e.g., *tell*) was used instead. Ideally, the numbers of tokens of each level of a linguistic predicting factor (e.g., a quotative that's reporting internal dialogue) is equal across participants. In reality, this is not usually possible with spontaneously produced speech. Thus, it's often necessary to set a minimum and maximum number of tokens for the cells. The cut-off used varies across studies depending on the number of both the tokens analyzed and the independent variables tested.

An alternative method of analysis is to count the number of times a form (e.g., *be like*) was used and then normalize the counts depending on the total number of words produced in the analyzed portion of speech (e.g., within a single interview). This method requires an especially large dataset and is most common within corpus linguistics, but it's also used by some sociolinguists (e.g., Buchstaller 2006). The two methods differ in the sorts of questions they can answer. The first is used to investigate the extent to which – when producing the target variable – the independent variables are correlated with the form that variable takes. The second is used to explore a token's frequency, which is also a relevant way of looking at sociolinguistic variables (and lexical variables in particular) since speakers who produce one of the variants 100 percent of the time when producing the variable may in fact produce fewer instances of the variant than someone who frequently uses the variable. These are two very different ways of looking at a similar question and they could potentially lead to very different conclusions. Thus, results from studies of the same variable that use the two methods should not be taken as equivalent but instead should be interpreted within the context of how the data were analyzed.

In many cases, sociolinguists build corpora for a specific project using some of the methods discussed in Sections 4.1.1. But, with a growing number of preexisting corpora freely available, there is an increasing number of studies that use preexisting data. Links to several freely available corpora are provided on the companion website.

Over the past two decades, there have been developments that make corpus data much easier to mine and analyze. One is the development of transcriptions tools, such as ELAN (Sloetjes & Wittenburg 2008), which allow the researcher to time-align the transcript with the sound file and include translations, speaker-specific tiers, and notes. Second, there are tools, such as LaBB-CAT (Fromont & Hay 2012), that are designed to extract sociolinguistic variables for analysis, and others, such as DARLA (Reddy & Stanford 2015) that can "transcribe" English and then, using FAVE (Rosenfelder et al. 2014), Prosodylab-Aligner (Gorman, Howell, & Wagner 2011), and the Vowels R package (Kendall & Thomas 2010), can force-align the transcriptions at the phoneme level and produce vowel plots. As a result of these developments, we can now analyze large numbers of tokens more quickly than ever before.

There are already a number of excellent resources describing data collection for a corpus, including discussions of how to elicit good interview data (Becker 2013; Rau 2013; Hill 2013; Hoffman 2014), what technology to use during the interview (De Decker & Nycz 2012; Hall-Lew & Plichta 2013), and best practices for transcription (Maclagan & Hay 2011). There are also excellent resources explaining the benefits of data preservation via corpus creation (Section 17 of Cohn, Fougeron, & Huffman 2012; Part III of Mallinson, Childs, & Van Herk 2013). In contrast, there are few resources geared toward sociolinguists that explain the nitty-gritty of setting up and maintaining a corpus. This is not particularly surprising given that the standards are constantly changing (don't you love technology?) and there can be challenges with security when using a server that is internet accessible. My recommendation is for all labs (or all suites of labs, as we have at the University of Hawai'i at Mānoa) to have an IT Specialist on staff so that the specialist can use their expertise to get something done in 10 minutes that would take someone like me 10 hours to do. Then, the linguists can have more time to spend on linguistics, and the IT Specialists can help with other cool stuff, like developing in-house software specific to the needs of your research team.

4.1.2. Reading tasks and wordlists

Compared to conversational data, reading passages have much more control because the content is controlled, word for word. Reading passages are most commonly used in sociolinguistics to examine phonetic variation in comparison with an analysis of the same variable from conversational data and/or wordlist data. Many scholars use preexisting reading passages, such as The Rainbow Passage or The North Wind and the Sun. However, depending on the language being investigated, there may not be a passage that is already commonly used. Also, preexisting passages may not contain some of the desired variables. Thus, in some cases, the passage must be designed.

When designing a reading passage, there are a few considerations to make:

1. If looking at a segmental variable, identify words that contain the target sound(s) in the position(s) of interest (e.g., word-medial). Setting up (and later analyzing) the task is easiest if all words belong to the same part of speech (e.g., they are all nouns) and if they have the same number of syllables. If two or more sounds are being compared, minimal pairs or near minimal pairs should be used, and stress should be controlled or balanced across all target sounds.

2. Identify a story that can link the words from (1) together. Multiple stories can be used if necessary, but note that if you are using a within-subjects design, conditions should be balanced across the stories.

3. If looking at a suprasegmental variable, identify sentence types of interest, and come up with a story in which multiple instances of the sentences types can be incorporated.

4. Write the passage, taking care to control all linguistic factors that might influence the variable. Target words should be balanced across any linguistic factors that are not controlled. Some linguistic factors to consider are likely patterns of stress and intonation (consider, e.g., position in a sentence) and surrounding environment.

5. If focusing on variables that occur at word boundaries (e.g., /r/-sandhi in English, *liaison* in French), it is critical that the passage be designed so that participants reading the passage will not pause before or after the target.

Another kind of reading task involves reading sentences or parts of sentences. The criteria for reading passages listed above apply, but a task that involves reading sentences or parts of sentences can be easier to set up since the sentences needn't form a coherent story. However, note that the order of sentence presentation should vary, either randomly (if using a small number of sentences and a large number of participants) or using a pseudorandom order (see Section 2.1.5). The inclusion of filler items may also be necessary.

When designing a wordlist, you can largely follow the same list of considerations as for a reading passage except that list intonation and distractor items should also be considered. When people read wordlists, it affects their intonation, and how it affects intonation depends on the speaker's language and dialect. Ensure that target words are in positions where they will be produced with the same intonation as one another, with filler words in the other positions. Distractor items can be used to hide the hypothesis being tested. If you wish to draw attention to the variable, then refrain from using distractor items.

Even with read speech, it is possible to manipulate the task in order to elicit different speech styles. For example, adding a distractor task to increase cognitive load can result in more phonetic reduction for some speakers, and asking them to repeat the utterance twice can result in a more careful style (Harnsberger, Wright, & Pisoni 2008). Social priming (see Sections 1.3.3 and 2.1.7) can also be used. Note that, as such manipulations are added, you should follow the guidelines for controlling and balancing discussed in Chapter 2.

4.1.3. Translation tasks: production

Translation tasks can be used to explore a number of different questions. Translation tasks used to investigate intelligibility are discussed in Section 3.2.8. Those discussed here focus on research questions surrounding production rather than perception.

In cases when languages are under-documented, a translation task, where participants translate words or sentences into the target language from a lingua franca, is sometimes used (see e.g., Lipski 2014). Because this can result in interference from the lingua franca, it is generally only used as a "first step" or in order to support corpus-based analyses.

However, there is some interesting untapped potential for sociolinguists to capitalize on the interference between language varieties. For example, there is evidence from perception that lexical access of words from one language is influenced by associated sociophonetic variants found in the prime, even when the prime word is a different language (Szakay, Babel, & King 2016). However, to my knowledge, an analogous study has not been conducted on production, despite the intriguing implications that would arise from looking at response times, word choices, and the linguistic variables observed in the participants' production of the target.

4.1.4. Picture naming

Picture naming has been an underused technique for production experiments in sociolinguistics, likely stemming from an overwhelming focus on highly literate populations. When working with non-literate populations, pictures are often used instead of text. Picture-naming tasks can also be helpful when studying a variable where spellings might influence realizations. Simple pictures can be used to elicit single word responses for work on phonetic variation, and more complex pictures can be used to elicit longer utterances. When longer utterances are elicited, a wider range of variables can be investigated.

This task can be used in a priming experiment, testing, for example, whether different groups of speakers are equally influenced by priming with a socially conditioned variable, or whether phonetic cues to the speaker's language or social background influence the effect of a syntactic prime.

4.1.5. Picture book narration

In order to elicit spontaneous connected speech, researchers can ask participants to narrate a picture book. Across the different subfields, there are a number of picture books that linguists commonly use. These include *A Boy, a Dog, and a Frog* by Mercer Mayer (used by Willis & Bradley 2008), *The Little Prince* by Antoine de Saint-Exupéry (used by Szakay 2008), and *Robot Dreams* by Sara Varon (used by Boyd et al. 2015).

Sometimes, it may be desirable to elicit certain sounds or words, or the researcher may wish to use a picture book that is culturally appropriate for the region where they are working. In such cases, an appropriate picture book may not already exist, in which case one would need to be created. For example, Katie Gao and Nozomi Tanaka created *The Cat Story* to investigate the link between language shift and marriage in three Yi villages in China (Gao & Tanaka 2015). After conducting a pilot study that identified lexical items with phonetic realizations that varied between the target dialects, Gao developed a story that contained these target items in order to determine which speakers of each dialect used the lexical item associated with the other dialect. For example, one of the words *ami*, meaning 'cat', differs in the tone (i.e., $a^{21}mi^{25}$ in the Miqie village but $a^{55}mi^{33}$ in the Geipo village). Through analyzing speakers' productions, Gao (2017) was able to demonstrate that there is surprisingly little shift away from the home village variety, even decades after moving to the other village. *The Cat Story,* along with the recordings and transcriptions of the resulting wordlist, are archived on Kaipuleohone, the digital archive for language materials at the University of Hawai'i at Mānoa.

4.1.6. Silent movie narration

An alternative to picture book narration is silent movie narration, where participants watch a short film without any sound and are asked to tell the story in their own words. This method is more appropriate than using picture naming if one wishes to elicit forms that depend at least partially on earlier information or utterances. For example, if you're looking at variability in whether a grammatical subject is overtly realized or not, then silent movie narration would be more appropriate than picture naming. Some scholars ask participants to narrate during their first watch of the film, but many play the entire film first and then ask the participant to narrate it, producing more fluent-sounding speech. Perhaps the most famous example of silent movie narration is the collection of studies in Chafe's (1980) edited volume, in which different researchers report results from elicitation using the same story. In addition to work on adults, the technique has been used to examine the speech of children. For example, Post and Nolan (2012) elicited simple constructions (e.g., *She's blowing bubbles*) from children using animated clips.

The film can be a combination of short clips depicting different scenes or it can be a short film with a coherent story. Another consideration is whether an animated film or a live action film should be used. The advantages of using live action include the ease of recording and the ability to incorporate aspects of life that are already familiar to the participant, including places and people known to the participant. However, when person recognition is undesirable or when the researcher would like to develop a single film to be used with many different populations, animation can be used. However, unless one has funds to pay for an animator or has the time and desire to learn to create simple animations (using e.g., Moovly), this option may not be feasible.

4.1.7. Enactment

Some researchers use (re)enactment to elicit spontaneous speech (e.g., Baker & Bradlow 2009). For these tasks, participants are either given explicit instructions on how to talk (e.g., "Say the following sentences as though you're talking with a good friend") or they're given a scenario (either verbally, read, or as a video) and they are asked either to retell the story in their own words or act out how they would respond in that situation. The advantages of this type of task are twofold: (1) they allow the researcher to control for topic while still eliciting spontaneous speech, (2) researchers can collect data for languages that they may not be able to speak fluently themselves, and (3) it's relatively easy and efficient. Enactment provides a way of observing speech styles that may be infrequent in traditional sociolinguistic interviews. For an example, Hardeman Guthrie (2013) used this technique to investigate *sajiao*, a gendered and sometimes stigmatized speech style used by speakers of Mandarin Chinese. The materials used in her study are available on the companion website, along with some sample data.

A disadvantage of enactment is, of course, that the participants are acting; it's not clear how closely their responses approximate what they would actually do in the situation. However, work comparing interactions with real and imagined interlocutors have found little difference between them (Scarborough, Brenier, Zhao, Hall-Lew, & Dmitrieva 2007). Still, it may be safest to view enactment as a "first step," with the expectation that future work will investigate the phenomenon in other ways.

4.1.8. Semi-structured games

Depending on the research question, designing semi-structured games for participants can be an excellent way to maintain control while eliciting spontaneously produced (i.e., non-read) speech. For example, in their work on prosody, Schafer, Speer, and Warren (2005) designed a game task where participants were provided with predetermined sentences they could use to move gamepieces around a board. Some of the sentences were ambiguous, requiring participants to disambiguate them through prosodic cues. The productions were analyzed acoustically and were played to different groups of participants to determine the extent to which listeners could use the prosodic cues to interpret the intended meaning. Other examples of semi-structured games used to investigate prosody include matching tasks with shapes of various colors (Swerts, Krahmer, & Avsani 2002) and a Clue-like game where a participant tries to determine the person, weapon, and location on the card of their co-participant (Experiment 2 in Hellmuth 2005). To add a social element to these types of tasks, one could explore dialectal differences, explore the extent to which prior familiarity with a game partner influences behavior on the task, or examine accommodation.

In another kind of semi-structured game, participants are provided with a map and are asked to give directions to an interlocutor (Scarborough et al. 2007). Scarborough et al. (2007) used the task to identify phonetic characteristics of foreigner-directed speech, but it could be used for a wide range of research questions. For more semi-structured games, see Sections 4.4.2 (Diapix task) and 4.4.3 (Tangram tasks) in the section on methods to study speech accommodation.

Explore the methods

wordlist
Llompart and Simonet (forthcoming)

enactment
Hardeman Guthrie (2013)

semi-structured games
Hellmuth (2005)

4.2. Surveys and questionnaires

A common method of data collection used by sociolinguists is a survey. Written surveys are often used alongside the collection of production and/or perception data, but sociolinguistics have also employed rapid and anonymous surveys (Labov 1966) and telephone surveys (Labov, Ash, & Boberg 2005) both of which can be used to elicit production data.

Good surveys are designed so that they do not lead participants to a particular response. (See Section 2.1.3.) In addition, a system of "checks and balances" can be included in order to test for consistency and dependability within responses from each participant.

Researchers using surveys should keep in mind that responses on surveys are highly susceptible to influence from mood, recent experiences, and a desire to present oneself in a positive light, even when completed by the most well-meaning participants. It is therefore important to remember during analysis and subsequent presentation that the survey results represent, at best, what participants believe and feel at the time they filled out the survey and that, in some cases, the results merely reflect what participants believed the researcher wanted to hear. Thus, many sociolinguists find surveys most useful as a way to collect speech samples (e.g., Labov 1966) or as preliminary or supplementary to other work.

There is a wide variety of types of survey questions, including rating tasks (Section 3.1.1), binary and multiple forced choice questions (Sections 2.1.2), semantic differential questions (Section 4.2.1), sentence completion and fill in the blank tasks (Section 4.2.2), grammaticality judgments (Section 4.2.3), and odd one out tasks (Section 4.2.4).

4.2.1. Semantic differential questions

Another method of eliciting specific lexical items is to ask semantic differential questions, such as "*What's the difference between a pond and a pool?*" The question draws less attention to the target sound than does a list of minimal pairs (Labov et al. 2005: 47) but it draws more attention than when the word arises spontaneously in spontaneous speech, making the method inappropriate for addressing some questions (Labov 2010: 266). In addition, the method normally involves use of the target words immediately following the experimenter's production of the same words, potentially biasing results. One way to get around this hurdle is to present the questions in a written format, which – in many cases – will increase the level of formality of the interaction. Thus, the method is inappropriate for some research questions and, like most methods, is most effective when triangulated.

4.2.2. Sentence completion and fill in the blank task

Typically, a sentence completion task involves providing the beginning of a sentence and asking participants to complete the sentence in their own words. This type of task is much more common in language acquisition research, but there is a great deal of potential for using sentence completion tasks in sociolinguistics. They can be used to investigate whether language or dialect use affects content (Ervin-Tripp 1967), to explore links between social information and syntactic structures, to test what social factors might prime the use of morphosyntactic variants, or to explore sociolinguistic variation (e.g., Csernicskó & Fenyvesi 2012). For example, in an investigation of dialectal differences in the Hungarian spoken in Hungary versus Subcarpathia (Ukraine), Csernicskó and Fenyvesi (2012) employed a number of techniques, including two different forced choice fill in the blank tasks, one that focused on lexical or phrasal variation and another that focused on variation in case marking. The latter of these is shown in Example 4.1, and the complete task is available on the companion website. In both cases the response was binary and forced choice. Comparing responses across different populations provides clues as to how the target variable patterns in formal speech styles.

(4.1)   select one: *légterét* or *légi terét*

A repülőgép-ek meg-sért-ett-ék Svájc _____.
the air.plane-PL PFX-violate-PAST-INDEF.3PL
    Switzerland _____.
"The airplanes violated Switzerland's (air space)."
(based on Csernicskó & Fenyvesi 2012. The standard form *légterét* and the non-standard form *légi terét* both mean "air space")

When eliciting open responses, some creativity in the design is required to ensure that productions include the variable of interest. The most appropriate set up will, of course, depend on the variable and language variety.

4.2.3. Grammaticality and acceptability judgments

Collecting grammaticality or acceptability judgments for sociolinguistic purposes can shed light on ideologies surrounding specific syntactic structures and how those ideologies might differ across different groups of individuals. And while responses on a binary forced choice task where participants indicate whether a sentence is grammatical or not might be enough information to address your research question, response times, reading times, and tracking eye movements during the judgment process may be even more revealing.

Other tasks that involve grammaticality or acceptability judgments include sentence correction – where participants are asked to provide a corrected version of an ungrammatical structure – and sentence selection – where participants are provided with several different possible structures and are asked to select the best-sounding one. When participants are run in dyads, these latter tasks can be used to collect production data that is often rich with a variety of different stance-taking mechanisms (see e.g., Higgins 2003), making it an excellent tool for analyzing variation in stances to linguistic variation. An example question from Higgins (2003) is shown in Example 4.2; the complete task is available on the companion website.

(4.2)

I am sorry for the botheration I have caused you.

OK   Not OK   Not Sure
Corrected Sentence: _____

How did you decide?
It sounds right/wrong   grammar rule   guess
Other method: _____
(based on Higgins 2003)

4.2.4. Odd one out task

In an odd one out task, participants are provided with a set of similar items and are asked to indicate which of the items is not like the others. The items can be made up of words (in order to target either specific sounds in the words or variation in the words' semantic or pragmatic meanings) or sentences (in order to target the interpretation of specific structures). The task is often done as a written task, as shown in Example 4.3, but, depending on the research question, could also be done using visual or auditory stimuli. Likewise, participants can be asked to read the words silently to themselves before responding, or they can be asked to read the words out loud.

(4.3)   Which word sounds different than the others? (circle one)
          pier   peer   pair
          (based on Hay, Drager, & Warren 2010)

Like grammaticality judgments, the odd one out task requires introspection on the part of the participant and can also be used to collect production data when responses are provided orally.

Explore the methods

Materials from the following studies are provided on the companion website: https://www.bloomsbury.com/cw/experimental-research-methods-in-sociolinguistics/

sentence completion and fill in the blank
Csernicskó and Fenyvesi (2012)

grammaticality/acceptability judgments
Higgins (2003)

odd one out task
Hay et al. (2010)

4.3. Example production experiment #1

As an example, I will step through an experiment based on work being conducted by one of my PhD students, Anna Belew. The experiment tests the extent to which social factors correlate with linguistic variation observed in the community and the degree to which members of the community are aware of the variation. In many speech communities, the first question could be answered through employing a sociolinguistic variationist analysis of naturalistic speech from sociolinguistic interviews or self-recordings. However, the researcher is not a speaker of this language, and the language is under-documented. Therefore, it is appropriate to use techniques that elicit less naturalistic speech for testing the hypothesis that social factors influence variation in this community, setting the stage for follow-up work on the variable.

Specifically, the sample experiment examines variation and awareness of variation in the use of plural markers in Iyasa, a Bantu language spoken in Cameroon that is essentially undocumented and is considered threatened (http://www.endangeredlanguages.com). With a younger generation that is increasingly moving to towns, Iyasa will potentially become endangered in the future, especially since – at an individual level – language shift is common when away from village life.

Anecdotal reports suggest that the forms of noun class markers in Iyasa are undergoing change, where younger speakers are producing variants of plural markers in select lexical items (e.g., *motorcycle* and *fork*) that are different from those used by older speakers. Specifically, the younger speakers are reported as generalizing plural morphology to these items although the words are traditionally used with singular markers even when in the plural. At this point, it's unclear whether this is a regular change in progress or a change that is a consequence of language shift, though, given the nature of the change, it seems likely to be the latter. Whether the variation is related with a speaker's gender or with living in one of the four Iyasa villages versus a larger and more linguistically heterogeneous city is unknown but is a question of interest. Therefore, the experiment is designed to (1) identify the variants used for the plural, (2) confirm whether the variation is conditioned by speaker age, (3) explore the extent to which speaker gender and locale relate to variation in the markers, and (4) examine whether community members are aware of any of the variation. A series of production tasks will be used to address these questions. The first three tasks are designed to elicit the plural markers used by the participant. The fourth task addresses the degree to which speakers are aware and/or have control of variation to the extent that they can produce it. Finally, the fifth task tests the extent to which the participants associate a form with a group of speakers, even if they're unable to produce or explicitly report on the variation themselves.

The first task that the speakers participate in is a movie narration task (Section 4.1.6). Participants are asked to watch a short (three-minute) animated movie. The target words (e.g., *motorcycle*) that are used with plural markers hypothesized to be undergoing change occur often in the film. The movie depicts cars parked in front of a small restaurant and two motorcycles pull up and park next to the cars. The drivers get off their motorcycles and enter the small building. A dog passes in front of the building. Upon receiving their food, the motorcycle riders are handed forks but ask instead whether they can have spoons. They see someone they know and talk for a bit before exiting the restaurant. Three dogs are in front of the building, and one of the dogs follows the motorcycle riders when they drive away. After watching the film once through, participants then rewatch the film and narrate the story as it unfolds. They are told to imagine that the person who will listen to the recording cannot see well, so they should try to provide as much detail as they can about the film they're seeing. After data collection is complete, each utterance of a target item will be coded according to whether the traditionally grammatical nominal marker was used or not, and this binary variable will be treated as the dependent variable during analysis. The independent variables to be tested are speaker age, whether or not the speaker was raised in a Iyasa area, and their score on the proficiency tests conducted after the main experimental tasks.

For the second task, participants are shown pictures and asked to name them (Section 4.1.4). In addition to the target words from the film (e.g., *motorcycles*), distractor items that were present in the film (e.g., *dog*) and additional targets and distractors are included (e.g., *canoes* and *fish*). The images are shown one at a time. Each image contains one type of item. For targets, two or more items are present in the image in order to elicit plurals, whereas distractors are sometimes shown as singular and other times with two or more. The order of the questions is fully randomized, and the task takes roughly 5–10 minutes to complete. The data will be analyzed using the same criteria as those outlined for the first task.

The third task is a sentence completion task (Section 4.2.2), where participants complete sentences about the pictures from the second task, with the noun and nominal marker. The task is a binary forced choice task, where participants must select the best option from the options provided. The results from this task will be compared with those from the first two tasks in order to see whether, when the traditional morphology for the target words is one of the options provided to young participants, they still select the tokens with a plural morpheme. The data will be analyzed using the same criteria as those outlined for the first task.

The fourth task is a picture-naming task with a twist: participants are shown a photograph of someone who they are told is a speaker of Iyasa, and they are asked how that person would say the word in Iyasa. There are four different photographs, corresponding to four different conditions: an older male (OM), and older female (OF), a younger male (YM), and a younger female (YF). The purpose of this task is to determine the extent to which speakers have awareness of any social patterning observed in the data of the first three tasks as well as the extent to which they have control over its production. Each participant takes part in all four conditions, and the order of the conditions is counterbalanced across participants. The items are identical to those used in the second task and only appear once in this task for each participant; by-item comparisons are done across participants. The dependent variable will be the same as in tasks 1–3 and the independent variables will be the age, gender, and village or town attributed to the person in the photograph, based on responses provided during a post-task questionnaire.

The fifth and final task is a matching task. Here, participants are played recordings of a single speaker producing the various forms elicited during the first two tasks. They are told that the speaker is imitating someone else talking, and their job is to figure out who is being imitated. The four pictures from the third task are shown on the screen and participants point to the person they believe is being imitated, with the researcher logging their response using the mouse. They are also given the option of reporting that the person being imitated is not a Iyasa speaker. The items are identical to those used in tasks 2 and 3 and, again, the order of the questions is fully randomized. Participants hear each target in only a single guise, so by-item comparisons must be done across participants. For half of the distractors, participants hear utterances that are ungrammatical; this way, the researcher can ensure that participants are not adopting a strategy of assigning all weird-sounding tokens to a particular photograph. The dependent variable will be the age of the person in the photograph, with the participant's age, home locale, and proficiency level treated as the independent variables.

Following the matching task, participants complete a questionnaire in which they indicate characteristics they attribute to the people in the photographs, such as where the person is from and how old they are, as well as rate their own proficiency. Then, participants complete a translation task to test proficiency more objectively.

4.4. Tasks for studying accommodation

While some of the tasks described above can be used to examine speech accommodation, they can also be used to examine a variety of other types of questions. In contrast, the tasks described in this section are best suited for studies that investigate accommodation because the nature of the tasks involve both teamwork and exposure to another speaker, increasing the chance that accommodation (either convergence or divergence) will occur.

Before deciding which methods to use, it is advised to first follow these general steps:

1. Determine the specific research question and/or hypothesis.

2. Decide what dialects/languages/variables you're going to focus on. This will be informed by your hypothesis/research question from 1.

3. Decide on primes (if relevant).

4. Decide what to measure: acoustic analysis vs. perceptual similarity.

Regardless of which of the methods are used to collect the data, there are several considerations during analysis, and plans for analysis should be made prior to data collection. For analysis, one option is to use an AXB task (Section 3.2.4), which compares listeners' perceptions of how similar the pre- and post-exposure tokens are to some stimulus. This task could be used to analyze accommodation at any level of the grammar and is appropriate as a holistic approach that focuses on variation that is salient to the listeners. Because it focuses on listener perceptions, using this method does not provide information about the specific ways in which speakers accommodate. To explore that, researchers must adopt other methods, which vary depending on the level of the grammar being investigated.

To explore accommodation at the phonetic level, acoustic analysis can be used. Acoustic phonetic analysis uses instrumental techniques to measure precisely what changed and by how much. Variables can be treated as gradient rather than discrete, and accommodation below a threshold of noticeability can be examined to determine whether accommodation occurs even when it's unlikely to be noticed by the listener. When measuring the acoustic distance between two realizations produced by the same speaker, no procedure for vocal tract normalization is necessary. However, if comparing two realizations by different speakers, normalization is recommended. The exception to this rule is if one is plotting the realizations within the context of the entire vowel space rather than running statistical analysis of formant values. Plotting unnormalized values within the context of the individual speakers' vowel spaces is especially appropriate if the realizations are massively different (e.g., the dialect of the talker is known to have much higher realizations of the target vowel than the participants' dialect area, and the talker's realizations are representative of their dialect).

To analyze accommodation of other variables (such as morphosyntactic variables), a coding scheme must be determined, which is often easier said than done. Ideally, coding schemes are designed prior to data collection but, often, they need to be altered or updated to fit the data at hand. Pilot data can help determine the appropriate coding system to use. Once the data are coded, a simple quantitative analysis can ensue (see Chapter 6).

Now that we've discussed techniques used to analyze data collected to investigate accommodation, we turn to methods used to elicit the data, including map tasks (Section 4.4.1), Diapix tasks (Section 4.4.2), Tangram tasks (Section 4.4.3), and imitation tasks (Section 4.4.4). Some additional tasks that can be used to investigate accommodation, such as interviews and semi-structured games, are discussed in Section 4.1.

4.4.1. Map task

The map task was developed by Anderson, Brown, Shillcock, and Yule (1984) as a way to elicit conversational data from teenagers. In this task, two participants are each given a map representing the same location but with some differing landmarks (see e.g., Pardo 2006, McCarthy, & Stuart-Smith 2013). One of the participants has a map with the path and goal marked, whereas the other participant only has landmarks on their map. (Note that this is not the same map task as that used in perceptual dialectology tasks.) The goal is for both participants to interact and, through working together, follow the path to the end. Example maps based on those used in Hellmuth (2014) can be found on the companion website, and links to other maps are also provided.

Beginning with the HCRC corpus, scholars have often chosen to have some kind of barrier between the interlocutors so that they were required to rely on vocal cues alone (Anderson et al. 1991). If interested in visual cues, such as gesture and facial expression, or if working with a signed language, video data should be collected and no barrier between participants should be used.

Advantages of this task include elicitation of a wide range of utterance types (e.g., declaratives, questions, exclamations) and the collection of connected speech. Disadvantages are that there are predetermined roles: the researcher determines which participant is the leader (i.e., which one gets the map with the path). When assigning roles, researchers should take care to follow the guidelines for balancing that were outlined in Chapter 2 as closely as is feasible. This may require asking participants to complete a demographic questionnaire prior to seeing up pairings of participants.

4.4.2. Dialogue-based picture matching (Diapix) task

Like a map task, a Diapix task (developed by Van Engan et al. 2010) involves two participants working together while looking at visual stimuli. In a Diapix task, each participant has a picture and they are asked to "spot-the-difference" between the two pictures. Since each participant cannot see the other person's picture, they must interact to complete the task. The advantages of the Diapix task are the same as the map task with the addition of avoiding predetermined roles for the participants. As explained by Baker and Hazen, "many aspects of speech during an interaction can be examined using the Diapix task – for example, global acoustic-phonetic characteristics, such as fundamental frequency range and mean, vowel space and speech rate, or discourse functions, such as uses of backchannels, hedges, and so forth" (2011: 756). But, given the collaborative nature of the task, it is probably most appropriate to examine speech accommodation, as done by Kim, Horton, and Bradlow (2011). Specific vowels (Van Engan et al. 2010), consonants (Baker and Hazen 2011), or other variables can then be examined during analysis.

An alternative to running the task with two participants is to use a monologic Diapix task, such as that used by Boyd et al. (2015). In a monologic Diapix task, participants interact with an imagined interlocutor.

For those wishing to conduct a Diapix task, preexisting pictures can be used. However, researchers targeting specific words, word classes, or sounds may need to create their own drawings. This has been done, for example, to target specific lexical items known to vary across different varieties (Stamp, Schembri, Evans, & Cormier 2016) and to elicit data from different languages (Kim et al. 2011); color images used by Stamp et al. (2016) are available on the companion website.

4.4.3. Tangram tasks

Another task that involves two speakers working together is the Tangram task described in Clark and Wilkes-Gibbs (1986). Tangrams come from a game in China, in which a square is cut into seven shapes, which can then be rearranged to make new shapes. Because the images merely resemble real-life objects, the task can be used to elicit hesitation and hedging strategies.

There are several different kinds of tasks that Tangrams have been used in. In one type of Tangram task, there is a director and a matcher. Both are provided with the same Tangrams, such as those shown in Figure 4.2, but the images are shown in a different order for each participant. Through communicating with one another, it is the matcher's job to put their Tangrams in the same order as those of the director's. Other scholars use Tangrams in matching tasks, where participants are asked to choose a picture based on their partner's description of a picture. Participants in this task alternate in whether they describe or identify a target Tangram (Bergmann, Branigan, & Kopp 2015). This role-shifting version of the task is especially well suited for examining accommodation.

Tangram tasks have also been used to investigate common ground and the extent to which descriptions change when a third party who is naïve to previous descriptions of the Tangrams enters the conversation (Yoon & Brown-Schmidt 2014).

Figure 4.2   Example Tangrams, shown in a different order to two interlocutors whose task it is to match the orders without looking at the other's Tangrams

4.4.4. Imitation/shadowing

In a shadowing task (also sometimes called an imitation task or mimicry), participants listen to words, sequences of words, or entire sentences and are asked to repeat them. The shadowing task is preceded by a pre-task (e.g., a wordlist), which provides a baseline. Then, the baseline production can be compared to the participant's production during the shadowing task to determine whether the participant shifted their realizations after exposure to the recorded voice.

For the shadowing task, the stimuli should be recorded using the standards set out in Section 2.1.1. But before recording can take place, the researcher must design the stimuli. For this description, I will focus on stimuli that are isolated words but longer utterances can also be used to explore prosody. Target words should be selected based on whether or not they include the target sound (aim for at least 10–20 words per target sound), and fillers should also be used. (See Section 2.1.3 for how to select fillers and Section 3.1.1 for an example.) While including fillers may not be entirely necessary when there is no clear pattern that can be identified among the target stimuli (e.g., you are interested in the entire vowel space), fillers could still be used in order to distract participants from the purpose of the task. In order to avoid ambiguity or misinterpretation of the word during listening, the word can be shown on the screen simultaneously with, or just prior to, playing the auditory stimulus. If this is done, then using fillers with spellings that "look weird" might serve you well since they would distract attention away from your hypothesis.

If using more than one voice, stimuli can be blocked by voice. Also, more words will be required since words should not be repeated across the different voices, and a Latin square design should be used (see Section 2.1.6). If there are not enough words in the target category, then use the same words across voices but play the voices in a different order for different participants.

When using isolated words during the shadowing task, many researchers opt to use the same lexical items in the pre- and post-tasks. This allows the researcher to make a direct comparison between the two productions, keeping phonological environment and lexical identity constant. A disadvantage of this approach is that realizations can shift as words are repeated, commonly undergoing more phonetic reduction (Baker & Bradlow 2009). If possible, the hypothesis should be created so that it is opposite to any expected effects of phonetic reduction (e.g., a shift toward a more peripheral vowel is hypothesized) when the same words are used pre- and post-task. If the shadowing task was conducted using headphones, then headphones should also be used during the pre-task; this is important since speakers could shift their realizations when wearing headphones compared to when they're not wearing any.

The instructions for this type of task may play a more important role than they do in some other kinds of tasks. That's because it's kind of a strange task: participants are asked to listen to someone say something and then repeat it, potentially leaving them to wonder why they aren't asked to read text or respond to images. In addition, participants may be unsure whether they are meant to imitate everything about the talker they hear or just say the words/sentences; this should be made clear. Walker and Campbell-Kibler disguised their hypothesis by misleading participants as to the purpose of the experiment, telling participants that "the goal of the repetition was to allow them to reflect on the differences between their own speech and that of the speaker they heard, and were specifically instructed therefore to not attempt to sound like the speaker they heard" (2015: 5). The extent to which this approach resulted in different behavior during the task remains unclear; Walker and Campbell-Kibler observed a shift in some variables even with these instructions, which they interpret as evidence that accommodation is indeed automatic and agency is not required. But the extent to which agency can play a role is still unclear and, as they suggest, direct linguistic input during a shadowing task may affect speech differently than other types of tasks (Walker & Campbell-Kibler 2015: 14). Much more work along these lines is needed to explore these questions. Also, note that when deception such as this is used, an exit survey should be conducted and an explanation of the deception (with the opportunity to withdraw from the study) must be provided after the participant has completed the experiment (see Section 2.1.3).

Explore the methods

Materials from the following studies are available on the companion website: https://www.bloomsbury.com/cw/experimental-research-methods-in-sociolinguistics/

map task
Hellmuth (2014)

Diapix task
Stamp et al. (2016)

imitation
Walker and Campbell-Kibler (2015)

4.5. Example production experiment #2

For this experiment, I will focus on variation and change observed in the vowel /ɛː/ in Swedish. Gross, Boyd, Leinonen, and Walker (2016) describe variation in young speakers' realizations that depends on a combination of the phonological environment, the speakers' city of origin (Gothenburg vs. Stockholm), and the speaker's background (whether or not the speaker is the child of an immigrant). The example experiment is designed to test whether the perceived immigrant background of the talker will affect a participant's convergence on the variants produced by that talker. The experiment is made up of three tasks: a pre-task (word-list), a map task (prime & test), and a post-task (test). Fluent speakers of Swedish from Gothenburg will be recruited for the experiment.

The task is a map task: the participant will hear a talker explain the route, but only some of the items mentioned by the talker can be found on the map. The participant is then expected to explain the route to a third confederate. While the participant is led to believe that both people they are interacting with are present in the other sound booths, they are hearing and seeing prerecorded stimuli. The stimuli are made up of prerecorded utterances and video of people's faces. They are prerecorded to maximize control across conditions. The auditory stimuli are sentences that contain words where the target sound occurs in the different phonological environments, and the word corresponds to an item on the participant's map. There are two sets of auditory stimuli: one in the Gothenburg guise and one in the Stockholm guise.

The video stimuli are composed of a face, prerecorded doing the task in a sound booth. The faces in the videos are Swedes of different backgrounds: one with an immigrant background (i.e., their parents or grandparents immigrated) and one without. Talker/face sex is controlled.

All participants listen and respond to the prerecorded stimuli described above, but they are led to believe that the recordings are produced live by other participants. Upon entering the lab, the experimenter greets the participant and tells them that the other participants have just arrived, are in the other sound booths, and are ready to begin once the participant is ready. The participant then enters their sound booth. The experimenter makes sure they have the headphones and head-mounted microphone properly adjusted and then leaves the booth, allowing the participant to complete the pre-task on their own. They are asked to press OK once the pre-task has been recorded. To enhance believability, the following message is displayed: "One of the other participants in your group is still completing the pre-task. Once everyone has finished, the experiment will automatically advance and you will hear the instructions for the next part of the experiment." After 30 seconds, the instructions are played. The instructions are in Swedish, but when translated into English are as follows: "Each participant in your group will be provided with a different version of a map. As a team, your job is to complete the route. All participants are fluent speakers of Swedish, and you are asked to only use Swedish on this task. Each of you has been randomly assigned a different role: Participant 1 is the Leader, Participant 2 is the Relayer, and Participant 3 is the Recipient. Each participant can see one participant and hear the other. You are Participant 2 (the Relayer) and can hear Participant 1 and see Participant 3. Your job is to relay the route from Participant 1 to Participant 3. When the red light on the webcam is on, your webcam is on and one of the other participants can see you. If you have questions for the experimenter, please open the sound booth door and ask them now. If you do not have questions, please click OK to begin." The participant is then shown a video. The person shown in the video will vary depending on condition. After 30 seconds, they will hear the stimuli described above. Individual participants will be exposed to only one of the conditions, so the auditory stimuli will either be played in the Gothenburg guise (where variation between speakers of different immigrant backgrounds was observed) or in the Stockholm guise (where no such difference was observed), and they will only see one of the faces. Once this task is complete, participants complete a post-task, where they re-record productions of the same lexical items as in the pre-task.

Note that an exit survey should be completed after the post-task, in order to determine whether the participant was aware of the deception. After this, participants must be informed of the deception and the reason for it, and they should re-sign a new version of the consent form that specifies that they still agree to participate. If they do not agree, their data must be destroyed.

4.6. Chapter summary

In this chapter, I have presented descriptions of tasks used in production experiments, some of which are heavily used by sociolinguists and others which are rarely used but may prove useful to explore some questions of interest to sociolinguists. This chapter is intended to:

- provide an overview of methods for exploring questions surrounding production, and
- suggest several directions for future work using the methods outlined.

For a description of how to visualize emergent patterns and run statistical tests, see Chapter 6.

Main points

- A variety of different methods can be used in a production experiment.
- Many of the best, most impactful studies are those that combine multiple methods.
- While some tasks are underused within sociolinguistics, they may present interesting opportunities to explore sociolinguistic research questions.

Further reading

Cieri, Christopher (2010). Making a field recording. In Marianna Di Paolo and Malcah Yaeger-Dror (Eds.) Sociophonetics: A student's guide. Routledge.
Clopper, Cynthia (2013). Experiments. In Christine Mallinson, Becky Childs, and Gerard Van Herk (Eds.) Data Collection in Sociolinguistics: Methods and applications. New York/London: Routledge, 151–161.

Cohn, Abigail C., Cécile Fougeron, and Marie K. Huffman (2012). *The Oxford Handbook of Laboratory Phonology*. Part V: Methodologies and Resources. Oxford University Press.

Krug, M. and J. Schlüter (2013). *Research Methods in Language Variation and Change*. Cambridge: Cambridge University Press.

Mallinson, Christine, Becky Childs, and Gerard Van Herk (2013). *Data Collection in Sociolinguistics: Methods and applications*. New York/London: Routledge.

Tagliamonte, Sali A. (2006) Analyzing Sociolinguistic Variation. Cambridge: Cambridge University Press.

Tagliamonte, Sali A. (2012) Variationist Sociolinguistics: Change, observation, interpretation. Malden/Oxford: Wiley-Blackwell.

Open frontiers

5

Crossover research faces the challenge of

satisfying the methodological requirements of more than one field,

but when it does successfully

it can explore fundamental theoretical issues in more than one domain

simultaneously.

– James M. Scobbie and Jane Stuart-Smith (2012: 611)

Sociolinguists have long been open to "thinking outside the box," adopting and adapting methods and theories from other disciplines and subfields in order to advance the understanding of the link between language and society. In terms of experimental work, many sociolinguists have argued in favor of crossover work, where sociolinguistics can both gain from and contribute to other fields and subfields, such as social psychology (Campbell-Kibler 2010b), laboratory/experimental phonetics and phonology (Hay & Drager 2007; Eckert & Podesva 2011; Scobbie & Stuart-Smith 2012; Warren & Hay 2012; Drager 2015), and psycholinguistics (Squires 2014); indeed, much of the work discussed in this book falls into one of these crossover categories.

However, we have only begun to scratch the surface, both in terms of the potential questions that could be asked and the methods that could be used. There are a number of methods that are woefully underused in sociolinguistics, despite being common methods in other areas. Some of these are relatively simple in their design, so they have been included in the previous two chapters. Others are much more complicated to design (and are not for the faint of heart), so I have dedicated chapter 5 entirely to them. For these methods, I highly recommend working closely with someone who has expert and current knowledge of the relevant best practices, and I present this chapter merely as a guide to give you enough knowledge to think up some cool research ideas and think through some of the appropriate issues and questions before your next meeting with the expert.

Explore the methods

Materials from studies that use the methods discussed in this chapter are available on the companion website: https://www.bloomsbury.com/cw/experimental-research-methods-in-sociolinguistics/

eye-tracking

Brouwer, Mitterer, and Hettig (2012)

mouse-tracking

Warren (2014)

EEG & ERP

Van Berkum, van den Brink, Tesink, Kos, and Hargoort (2008)

ultrasound

Lawson, Stuart-Smith, and Scobbie (2014)

5.1. Eye-tracking

Tracking eye movements as a way to gain insights into cognition was first pioneered by Cooper (1974) and was later popularized by Tanenhaus, Spivey-Knowlton, Eberhard, and Sedivy (1995). Eventually, the method came to be known as the visual world paradigm (Allopenna, Magnuson, & Tanenhaus 1998). The idea behind the paradigm is that tracking a participant's eye movements provides insight into their visual attention. In addition to being influenced by visual information, visual attention is also influenced by auditory information. The visual world paradigm is common in psycholinguistics, addressing a large range of questions such as identifying the timecourse of processing phonological, semantic, and visual shape information (Huettig & McQueen 2007) and the extent to which speakers of different languages vary in which syntactic-semantic categories are processed during speech planning prior to production (Hwang & Kaiser 2014). Please see Huettig, Rommers, and Meyer (2011) for an overview of the different kinds of questions and tasks.

In perception tasks, an auditory stimulus accompanies the visual stimulus; in production tasks, only visual stimuli are normally presented. Generally, participants complete an active task of some kind (e.g., a scene description or click on a response), even though eye movements are the dependent variable of interest. However, there is also work that tracks gaze while the participant listens to stimuli that they do not actively respond to (e.g., Kamide, Altmann, & Haywood 2003). Given the risk of non-attention and the benefits of knowing something about the participants' interpretation when analyzing eye movements, sociolinguists may want to wait to use the more passive method until more is known about which research questions, stimuli, and tasks this type of passive participation is most appropriate for.

Some of the existing work from psycholinguistics has potential for interesting crossovers with sociolinguistics (e.g., Brouwer et al. 2012; Trude & Brown-Schmidt 2012; On Yoon & Brown-Schmidt 2014), diving further into the social realm than the work currently goes. For example, Trude and Brown-Schmidt's (2012) work on whether and when listeners' perception of words is influenced by dialectal features of the talker is linked with work on the processing and intelligibility of non-native varieties (Section 1.3.2). Likewise, the work in Brouwer et al. (2012) raises questions about what social factors might influence the processing of phonetically reduced tokens and the processing of vernacular forms. For example, would different behavior be observed across listener groups that – due to the dialects they speak – exhibit differences in whether and how forms are reduced? And would listeners be sensitive to variation across talkers from these regions? Some examples of sociolinguistic work that has used the visual world paradigm include Koops, Gentry, and Pantos (2008), McGowan (2011), and D'Onofrio (2015). As eye-tracking technology continues to become more user friendly and as more sociolinguists become familiar with the best practices of the visual world paradigm, I anticipate seeing an increase in the number of sociolinguistic studies that use it.

One area within sociolinguistics that would benefit from the use of eye-tracking is work on speech accommodation, exploring questions around the automaticity of accommodation and the roles of social information and common ground. While the vast majority of visual world studies test participants individually, some studies investigate eye movements during an interaction, either with a confederate (Hanna, Tanenhaus, & Trueswell 2003), in an assigned role (On Yoon & Brown-Schmidt 2014), or in a collaborative game (Brown-Schmidt, Gunlogson, & Tanenhaus 2008).

In order to determine how likely it is that participants will look at specific regions or objects at different points in time, researchers can consider the shifts in gaze (known as *saccades*) or the periods of time spent gazing at an object (known as *fixations*). The analysis normally considers the proportion of fixations or saccades to a region of interest out of all possible regions of interest within a given time frame (e.g., a 200ms frame). The decision to analyze saccades versus fixations is not as trivial as it may initially seem. As explained by Tanenhaus and Trueswell (2006), "because each fixation is likely to be 150–250 ms, the proportion of fixations in different time windows is not independent. One way of increasing the independence is to restrict the analysis to the proportion of new saccades generated to pictures within a region of interest" (2006: 869).

Visual stimuli in experiments that use the visual world paradigm normally include targets, competitors, and distractors. Targets are the items that correspond with items in the auditory stimuli (for perception experiments) or that are to be produced (for production experiments). Competitors are those that are expected to compete with the target for visual attention. The competition can stem from similarities in phonological form (e.g., *beaker* and *beetle*), rhyme (e.g., *beaker* and *speaker*), semantics (e.g., *beaker* and *container*), or any other factors shared with the target that may attract visual attention. (When considering social factors, the possibilities seem almost endless!) In addition to targets and competitors, distractors are also used. These items are included in order to help conceal the hypothesis as well as to create more variability in gaze prior to the onset of the target in the auditory stimuli or the relevant planning during speech production.

The simplest designs usually have four items on the screen (one target, one competitor, and two distractors) that are maximized for distance (see Figure 5.1) though fewer items can also be used. However, avoid placing items too close together, if possible; compared to items placed at maximal distance from one another, placing visual stimuli close together necessitates an even more precise calibration and it complicates analysis.

In perception studies, the participant's task is often to click on the image that corresponds with what they hear. However, it is also possible to use more complicated tasks, such as dragging and dropping an item from one part of a scene to another or adding, deleting, or rearranging images to complete a semi-structured game.

As discussed in Section 3.2.2, the use of visual stimuli necessitates making a decision between using images and text. Both are possible using the visual world paradigm: using text has the benefit of being able to use a wider range of words (including abstract concepts that are not easily represented in images) whereas images have the benefit of being used with pre- or non-literate populations and, importantly, they may also avoid privileging phonological processing. Whatever type of visual stimuli are used, it is important to consider how those stimuli might influence visual processing independent of any linguistic processing. See Section 2.1.1 for further discussion of some of these considerations.

In addition to the visual stimuli intended to attract gaze, other visual stimuli (such as primes), a fixation cross that is intended to "reset" the participant's gaze between trials, and auditory stimuli can also be used. The order in which participants are exposed to these various stimulus types and the time between each type require careful consideration, and decisions should be made within the context of the specific stimuli being used. For example, whether the target, competitor, and distracters are shown on the screen prior to exposure to an auditory stimulus depends at least partially on whether that auditory stimulus is a long utterance with the target at the end (in which case presentation of the auditory and visual stimuli could be simultaneous) or is a single word (in which case presentation of the visual stimuli most often precedes presentation of the auditory stimulus). In cases when an influencing factor corresponds with the start of a clip (e.g., talker sex), it may be necessary to present the visual stimuli prior to presentation of the auditory stimuli so that unrelated biases can be identified.

When designing the experiment, it is also important to consider how gaze will be analyzed; analysis involves splitting the time spent on each question into smaller chunks within which proportion of new looks to (or fixations on) the target are measured. But how long are those chunks? Answering this during experiment design will help guide decisions as to the appropriate duration for stimuli and when various stimuli should be presented in relation to one another. So far, sociolinguists have opted to use relatively large chunks, treating, for example, the time immediately following the disambiguation point to the time of the response as a chunk.

In contrast, psycholinguists generally focus on much smaller chunks (e.g., 20ms) and consider the time prior to the disambiguation point as well as time well after. Using smaller chunks provides more detail and would often be beneficial in addressing sociolinguistic research questions.

Another thing to consider are the areas of interest (AOIs), which – with most modern eye-tracking equipment – are defined prior to data collection. AOIs are the regions in the visual scene that are considered distinct from one another. A single size and shape can be used for all of the items, or the researcher can set item-specific AOIs that, for example, follow the outer contours of each item. When there are only four items and they are maximally distributed, the size and shape of the AOIs is often controlled. For scenes, the size and shape of the AOIs are more likely to vary across items but, relevant for cases when items appear close together, AOIs cannot overlap.

In addition to the main experiment and any pre-task or practice task that might be included, the equipment must be calibrated for every participant. Proper calibration increases the likelihood that the participants' gaze is tracked accurately, despite individual differences in eye placement, shape, and movements. During calibration, participants should be instructed to complete the task (e.g., watch a dot move around on a screen) without trying to anticipate the movements. While glasses and soft contacts do not usually pose a problem, eye make-up and false lashes can interfere with tracking gaze; for experiments conducted in the Tracker Lab at UH Mānoa (a lab co-directed by Amy Schafer and Theres Grüter), participants are asked to arrive without make-up and eye make-up remover is kept in the cabinet, just in case. In some cases, participants cannot be calibrated, and their data must be discarded before analysis.

If you are going to purchase eye-tracking equipment, it's worthwhile to do some research into which system is best for you. Eye-tracking equipment has greatly improved in ease of use since the inception of the technique, simplifying calibration of the equipment to each participant's eyes and gaze as well as improving ease of data analysis. In the LAE Labs at UH Mānoa, we have the SMI Experiment Suite, with Experiment Center and BeGaze. However, this system is not appropriate for all questions and contexts, so researchers must determine what the best system is for their questions before making what is a fairly large investment. For example, a portable system would be more appropriate if wishing to run an eye-tracking experiment in the field, and you may prefer a different system if you are interested in tracking reading times. For those looking for a low budget option, a series of video cameras can be used to track gaze. This involves much more intensive coding after data collection and it is only appropriate for some tasks, such as those that involve real-life objects placed a far enough distance from one another to enable straightforward coding. Since person hours are much higher for this low budget option, it is unfeasible for many researchers.

In order to clarify some of the points made above, we now turn to a sample experiment. The sample experiment tests whether a talker's gender influences how words are processed. So, in terms of gaze, we are testing whether listeners are more likely to gaze at a female-associated target or competitor than a male-associated one when listening to a female talker. Note that this experiment has not actually been conducted; this is a sample experiment that Amy Schafer and I designed in order to demonstrate the paradigm for our co-taught graduate level class *Sociolinguistics, Psycholinguistics, and Eyetracking*.

In the sample experiment, two voices are used – one male and one female – and both male- and female-associated targets are used. Target and competitor words have identical first syllables but are disambiguated after the first syllable (e.g., *necklace* and *necktie*). There are also two fillers (e.g., *cup* and *sofa*). In order to give the listener plenty of time to extract social information from the auditory stimulus, we use a carrier phrase ("*Look at the ____*"). This is also done so that we can track gaze prior to the disambiguation point, identifying any bias toward one of the images that is unrelated to our research question. When the target is necklace, participants hear "*Look at the necklace*" and are shown four images: a target (*necklace*), a competitor (*necktie*), and two fillers (*cup* and *sofa*), as shown in Figure 5.1. If this item is in the matched/congruent condition, then participants hear the stimulus in a woman's voice whereas they hear it in a man's voice in the unmatched/incongruent condition. The hypothesis is that, upon hearing *neck-*, participants will be more likely to gaze at the image that is stereotypically associated with the same sex that is attributed to the voice.

The placement of the target and competitor are balanced across items, and four lists are used with different combinations of targets and talkers. For example, there are two lists where *necklace* is the target: one where it is in the congruent condition and one where it is in the incongruent condition. There are also an additional two lists – one for each condition – for which *necktie* is the target. And there are lots of other items (e.g., *nail gun* vs. *nail polish*, *laundry bin* vs. *lawnmower*) included in each list.

Upon hearing the auditory stimuli, participants are asked to click on the image that corresponds to the last word of the sentence. Data from correct trials are analyzed.

Note that the sample eye-tracking experiment is a simple one in order to demonstrate just how much attention to detail needs to go in to the design for even the simplest experiment. Adding more conditions or

Figure 5.1 Sample visuals from the example eye-tracking experiment for an item in which participants hear *Look at the necklace.* The target is *necklace* and the competitor is *necktie*. The coffee cup and sofa are unrelated distractors. Anticipatory looks to the necklace are predicted for the condition when the talker a woman, whereas anticipatory looks to the necktie are predicted when the talker is a man

using a more complicated task (e.g., moving and dropping items) will complicate the design process further.

Now let's skip ahead to pretending that we've already run the experiment. At this point, the data output is extremely overwhelming with a row for every fixation of every participant; a single participant answering only six questions can yield over 70 rows of data. The exact number of rows will vary across items and participants since different participants vary in the amount of time they spend gazing at the visual stimuli and answering each question, but you can compare the possibility of 70 rows in an eye-tracking experiment to a forced-choice discrimination task, where the same six questions provide six rows of data.

At this point, the data require some massaging to get them into a useful format. Having a row for every fixation is great, but it isn't very helpful in terms of visualizing gaze (which varies across participants) within small chunks of time (that are constant across participants). So the data are then converted from one row per fixation to one row per chunk of time (e.g., 20ms) specifying the AOI being fixated upon during that time window or information that there is no fixation during that period. The process of converting the data into this preferred format is commonly

Figure 5.2   Fake data from the incongruent condition. The line at x=0 indicates the disambiguation point

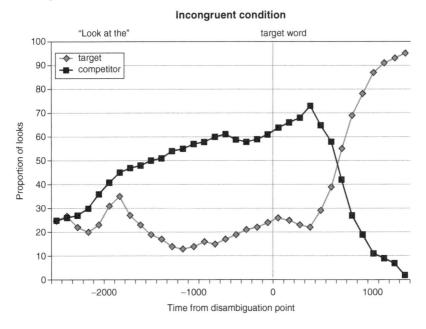

Incongruent condition

"Look at the"   target word

- target
- competitor

Proportion of looks

Time from disambiguation point

done with the help of R scripts, and there are even R packages (e.g., eyetrackingR designed by Jacob Dink and Brock Ferguson and available at http://www.eyetracking-r.com) designed for this purpose. Because different systems produce different output and the output is further affected by the experiment design, I will not cover the specifics of the relevant R scripts here; this is something to discuss with your resident expert.

Once my data are set up appropriately, I use my new and improved spreadsheet to calculate the proportion of looks to the competitor and target for each window duration. Note that the first look to a region of interest should not be treated the same as a fixation; in cases when they are both analyzed, they should be analyzed separately. I then plot the data separately for the congruent (Figure 5.3) and incongruent (Figure 5.2) conditions, though I am especially concerned with the proportion of looks to the target for the incongruent condition.

In order to make the plot interpretable, it's helpful to provide a marker for the disambiguation point (here, a line part-way through the target word) and to provide the rest of the context (e.g., "Look at the") as well as an indication of time in milliseconds. Duration is averaged across the stimuli though care should be taken during design to control the duration before and after the disambiguation point. Note that switches in gaze are not instantaneous with exposure to the target; the exact duration of the

Figure 5.3   Fake data from the congruent condition. The line at x=0 indicates the disambiguation point

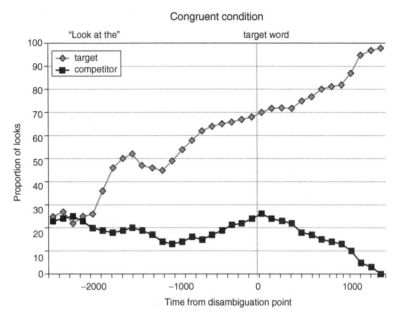

delay can vary across participants and tasks but, for a task like this, the delay is often around 250ms after the disambiguation point.

As with all experiments, when writing up the results from an eye-tracking experiment, be sure to include descriptions of all of the methodological decisions made, providing justification if and when they diverge from common practice in the psycholinguistic literature that uses the visual world paradigm.

5.2. Mouse-tracking

The equipment required for eye-tracking is highly specific and very expensive. Most eye-tracking systems are also extremely cumbersome, making them impractical to bring to a fieldsite. Mouse-tracking is a cheaper, more mobile option. As it is not as sensitive as eye-tracking, it cannot be used to answer all research questions. However, it is sensitive enough to be useful in answering some questions of interest to sociolinguists. For example, Squires (2014) used mouse-tracking during self-paced reading to investigate processing standard vs. non-standard syntactic forms, and Warren

(2014) examined the degree to which segmental and suprasegmental socio-linguistic variables, together, affect the interpretation of an utterance.

Mouse-tracking is similar to eye-tracking in that it can be used with different types of tasks. Likewise, a large amount of control and counter-balancing is required in order to obtain meaningful results. While partici-pants' handedness is important to note for most experimental work, it is especially important and is often controlled when using this paradigm. In addition, it is necessary for participants to begin movement early, before they've made their final response decision. This is natural with eye move-ment but sometimes must be encouraged when tracking mouse move-ment. Thus, many scholars begin with an explanation that participants can begin their responses immediately, and that they should work quickly and follow their intuitions. Some scholars also speed up the task, with a "please respond more quickly" message appearing if the participant has not responded within a predetermined amount of time.

In contrast with eye-tracking, no special hardware is required for mouse-tracking; all you need is a mouse and a computer. There are sev-eral different software programs available. MouseTracker is popular and is freely downloadable from http://www.freemanlab.net/mousetracker. Also, if a mouse doesn't seem like quite the right tool, other options are also possible. For example, rather than asking participants to use a mouse, Hesson and Shellgren (2015) opted for an electronic drawing tab-let, which was synchronized with mouse movement on the researchers' computer.

The most common method of analysis in mouse-tracking studies is to analyze trajectories by focusing on the area under the curve (see Freeman & Ambady 2010). However, other more sophisticated measures are also available. For many questions that sociolinguists are likely to use this method to answer, it will be desirable to time-align tracks with the content of the utterance, indicating on the plot when the disambigu-ation point or difference between guises was shown. Hehman, Stolier, and Freeman (2014) provide an excellent tutorial on how to analyze data this way using MouseTracker.

5.3. Event-related potentials

Electroencephalography (EEG) is a method of analyzing brain activity through recording the brain's electrophysiological response to a stimu-lus. One way of analyzing EEG data (and the only way that I'm aware of that has been used within sociolinguistics) is the event-related potential (ERP) technique. The technique involves using time-locked stimuli, and the brain's responses are output as waveforms. Typically, multiple responses are averaged within a condition in order to compare, across conditions, the differences between the (averaged) waveforms. EEG has better temporal resolution than some other measures of brain activity (e.g., fMRI), though other methods tend to have better spatial resolution, especially for some brain regions.

When running these experiments, electrodes are placed on different parts of the participants' scalp and the participants then passively listen to speech while brain activity is measured. Contrasts are set up in the stimuli so that a change induces brain activity. As a simple example, if the stimuli contain [ba ba ba ba ba da da da da] a measurable shift in the EEG should occur following the shift from [ba] to [da].

The time-aligned EEG signal is averaged across experimental conditions (e.g., one with a [ba]-[da] transition and one with all [ba]-[ba] tokens), resulting in what are known as ERP components (i.e., stereotyped electrophysiological responses to a stimulus). It is these components that are believed to provide insight into the brain's activity to certain kinds of stimuli. One of the most heavily studied is the N400, which, when the negativity is greater, may indicate a higher level of difficulty in integrating conflicting information (see e.g., Camblin, Gordon, & Swaab 2007). Thus, we might predict that switches and incongruent stimuli will result in greater negativities.

There are very few sociolinguistic studies that measure EEG. One of the few is by Dufour, Brunelliére, and Nguyen (2013), who examined Southern French listeners' sensitivity to the sociolinguistic variant [o], a variant which exists in Standard but not Southern French. They found that listeners were sensitive to the variation but that detection occurred later than it did when the switch was to a sound native to the region. These results raise a number of interesting questions about the role of exposure, salience, and perceived standardness on the brain's physical response to sociolinguistic variation. There is also work examining the extent to which the content of a sentence induces surprisal when at odds pragmatically with the social characteristics attributed to a talker (Van Berkum et al. 2008). The results are subtle but the effect is in the expected direction: incongruence between the talker and the content result in an N400 effect. Follow-up work suggests that the extent to which such top-down expectations influence processing of speech is related to the participant's tendency or ability to empathize (van den Brink et al. 2012). Finally, Loudermilk (2015) examined the extent to which implicit attitudes as measured using an IAT (see Sections 1.3.1 and 3.1.4) correlated with results from ERP components. The experiment is more complex than the others and the results are fairly inconclusive, but they may suggest that ERP was influenced by a combination of the speaker's dialect and the participants' behavior on the IAT.

The equipment that is used to run ERP experiments is highly specialized and expensive, though not nearly as expensive as that used for fMRI or MEG. They also require a large amount of attention on the part of the experimenter during the data collection process itself in to order to place the electrodes correctly and establish proper contacts; in contrast, MEG doesn't have this problem. The experimenter should pay attention to the output (shown in real time on a computer screen) throughout the data collection process to ensure accurate measurements. For an introduction to selecting the proper resolution, collecting and analyzing ERP data, and setting up an ERP lab, please see Luck (2014) and the associated online-only content.

5.4. Experiments for working with children

Anyone with children will understand when I say that it can sometimes be a challenge to get young children to sit still, focus on a task, and not fidget with something new (like recording equipment) in their environment. Thus, researchers interested in child language acquisition often need to be extremely creative and patient in order to collect the data they need while also keeping the child entertained. Despite these challenges, working with children can be a pleasure (Khattab & Roberts 2010).

A great deal of the sociolinguistic work on children's speech involves corpora of spoken language (reviewed in Labov 2012), examining when sociolinguistic variation is acquired and the degree to which a child's peers influence their production. While the criteria for working with adults (see Chapter 2) still apply, there are a few extra considerations when creating a corpus of children's speech. For example, where is the mic placed? Some scholars have created exciting play-vests that have a microphone and recorder sewn in and, now with wireless equipment, the recorder needn't even be in the vest.

However, just as with adults, spontaneous speech data are not appropriate for every question and may not accurately represent the child's knowledge (Wagner, Clopper, & Pate 2014: 1065). For example, infants who cannot yet speak are still sensitive both to dialectal differences

(Butler, Floccia, Goslin, & Panneton 2011) and to relationships between the genders of faces and talkers (Patterson & Werker 2002). Experimental paradigms can also help answer questions about perception and the acquisition of attitudes by children, and can be used to elicit forms that rarely occur in natural speech. Some of the same experimental paradigms can be used with children as with adults as long as they are appropriately simplified and made fun. For example, researchers can use categorization tasks that involve puppets rather than labels (e.g., Wagner et al. 2014), mirroring tasks that incorporate popular stories (Nathan, Wells, & Donlan 1998), and visual stimuli that depict pictures of popular characters.

Even the best-designed, most entertaining experiments are likely to end up with some child "losing it" during the course of running the experiment. If this happens, don't take it personally: anticipate a high rate of data loss and build it into your initial timeline.

5.5. Ultrasound

Ultrasound is increasingly being used to investigate sociophonetic research questions (Lawson, Scobbie, & Stuart-Smith 2011; De Decker & Nycz 2012) and, in some cases, has helped to identify sociolinguistic variation that went undetected in the acoustics. Just as with eye-tracking, it is recommended that scholars new to this method work closely with a phonetician who is already highly familiar with the method before branching out on one's own.

Ultrasound can be used for visual confirmation or exploration of lingual articulations and, when conducted properly, it can be used to collect quantitative articulatory data of tongue movements and positions. In contrast with some other methods for studying articulation, it is inexpensive, non-invasive, portable, and the entire tongue can be imaged (Davidson 2012: 484). This makes it an attractive choice for examining articulation in the field. For a discussion of using ultrasound to study understudied languages in the field, see Gick (2002). For a discussion of risk associated with the technique, see Epstein (2005).

Handheld probes are placed against the skin to collect qualitative data. To collect quantitative data, a headset should be used to keep the probe in place across the different utterances produced (Davidson & De Decker 2005). Despite the somewhat imposing nature of the headset, Scobbie,

Stuart-Smith, and Lawson (2008) found that it was still possible to elicit casual speech styles.

In order to time-align the visual and audio recordings, video can be streamed directly to a camera or computer. Some machines are capable of capturing a faster frame rate if recorded internally to the machine, but then alignment of the audio and visual data must be done after data collection. (Space on the ultrasound machine may also be very limited; be sure to pilot the task in advance of data collection.) Therefore, many researchers collect high quality sound files and time-align them with the images using computer software (e.g., a Canopus ADVC 1394 audio/video capture card on a computer collecting both the visual and audio data) at the time of recording.

Depending on the research question, prompts are designed, keeping in mind the requirements of balance and control (Chapter 2) and for particular tasks (Chapter 4).

For analysis, tongue contours can be traced automatically, using software such as EdgeTrak, and then altered manually. Some analysts then use smoothing spline modeling to compare tongue shapes (see e.g., De Decker & Nycz 2012). Davidson (2012) and Scobbie et al. (2008) provide excellent introductions to using ultrasound, and all of the techniques they discuss would be appropriate for work in sociophonetics.

5.6. Chapter summary

The methods discussed in this chapter are exciting additions to the range of tools sociolinguists already use. Specifically, this chapter provides introductions to:

- eye-tracking
- mouse-tracking
- EEG/ERP
- experiments with children
- ultrasound

Part of the promise of these methods comes from their sensitivity, but this also means that extreme care must be taken in implementing them and interpreting results from experiments that use them. Thus, sociolinguists should seek to gain proper training (beyond what can be garnered from reading this book) before employing them.

Main points

- Generally speaking, the more sensitive the measure, the more control is necessary.

- If you don't need the more sensitive measure to address your research question, use a simpler experimental method instead.

Further reading

Cohn, Abigail C. and Cécile Fougerson, and Marie K. Huffman (2012). *The Oxford Handbook of Laboratory Phonology*. Oxford: Oxford University Press.

Hehman, Eric, Ryan M. Stolier, and Jonathan B. Freeman (2014). Advanced mouse-tracking analytic techniques for enhancing psychological science. *Group Processes and Intergroup Relations* 1–18. DOI: 10.1177/1368430214538325.

Huettig, Falk, Joost Rommers, and Antje S. Meyer (2011). Using the visual world paradigm to study language processing: A review and critical evaluation. *Acta Psychologica* 137(2): 151–171.

Khattab, Ghada and Julie Roberts (2010). Working with children. In Marianna Di Paolo and Malcah Yaeger-Dror (Eds.) *Sociophonetics: A student's guide*, 163–178. Abingdon/New York: Routledge.

Luck, Steven J. (2014). *An Introduction to the Event-Related Potential Technique*, 2nd edition. Cambridge, MA: MIT Press. https://mitpress.mit.edu/books/introduction-event-related-potential-technique-0.

Scobbie, James M., Jane Stuart-Smith, Eleanor Lawson (2008). Looking variation and change in the mouth: Developing the sociolinguistic potential of Ultrasound Tongue Imaging. Unpublished Research Report for ESRC Project RES-000-22-2032. Downloaded 13 December 2016 from https://core.ac.uk/download/pdf/41504.pdf

Stone, Maureen (2005). A guide to analyzing tongue motion from ultrasound images. *Clinical Linguistics and Phonetics* 19(6/7): 455–501.

Tanenhaus, Michael K. and John C. Trueswell (2006). Eye movements and spoken language comprehension. In Matthew J. Traxler and Morton A. Gernsbacher (Eds.) *Handbook of Psycholinguistics,* 2nd edition. Amsterdam/Boston: Elsevier, 863–900.

Statistics for experimental sociolinguistics

6

Chapter outline

*The statistical analysis of quantitative data is often seen as an onerous
task that one would rather leave to others.*

– Harald Baayen (2008: viii)

For some, statistics is extremely overwhelming. The many choices and the
equations and then – *groan* – the use of R, it can be a lot to deal with.
However, statistical analysis can actually be a lot of fun. Think of it like
playing with your data: you've worked hard to get the experiment design
just so, and you've finally run all of the participants you need, and now
it's time to play! Hooray! Setting aside a good chunk of time to play with
the data is important; even after you're extremely familiar with statistical

analysis, you'll get far more enjoyment out of the whole process if you aren't rushed.

Learning how to use R is much the same. View it like a puzzle in which you get to figure out what each little bit of code does. (Relax, if you're a linguist, you're already good at this sort of task. We've been training to do this sort of puzzle-solving since Linguistics 101.) I've found, both through my own experience and in teaching R to students, that learning how to use R is the most fun when working with your own data. So while it makes sense to begin by using the sample spreadsheet and R script I created (both of which are freely downloadable from the companion website), I also encourage you to try each of the steps with your own data soon after running the sample script. After you start working with your data is when you'll really start to make sense of things.

In this chapter, I'll present some of the most commonly used statistical methods, stepping through how to pick the right one for your data and how to use R to run the different tests. The sample R script follows the same order as this book (and in many cases, uses the identical code) so that you can follow along in R as you read this chapter.

The vast majority of work in experimental sociolinguistics is analyzed using some form of regression model. In this chapter, I cover three types: linear, logistic, and ordered regression, all with mixed effects. These are presented at the end of the chapter, after a brief introduction to R (Section 6.1), some instruction on creating simple plots in R (Section 6.2), and discussion of some simpler statistical techniques (Section 6.3).

6.1. A crash course in using R

6.1.1. Setting up a spreadsheet

The program known as R is powerful and wonderful… and extremely literal. Not all things will be interpreted by R in the same way that many humans would intuitively interpret them. Here are some things I suggest doing and avoiding when setting up your spreadsheet since they can help you avoid a big headache later and should help make the learning curve with R a little less steep.

Before you've even finished setting up your experiment, it's a good idea to think about what you want your final spreadsheet to look like. Doing so can help you troubleshoot the design, code for additional factors you might otherwise fail to consider, and check – during test runs – that the program you're using to run the experiment is indeed inputting all of the information that you want.

Set up your spreadsheet so that each datapoint has its own row. This means that a single participant will have many, many rows, one for each token. For some experiments (like a forced-choice identification task or a production task that measures the interval of time between the stimulus and the response), there should be one row per stimulus. In other types of experiments (e.g., eye-tracking and, in some cases, rating tasks with several questions per stimulus), there are multiple rows for a single stimulus.

When I set up a spreadsheet, I like to keep columns that contain descriptive information about the stimuli all near each other, response and response-related columns all near each other, and columns with participant demographic information all near each other. Failing to do so won't break R, but it will probably make your life easier down the road. Demographic information about the participant should be "copied down" with the participant's unique identifier. When you do this, double-check that it has all been copied properly. If you have information in two separate sheets (e.g., one for responses and one for participant demographic information), there are ways to merge these documents in R. However, I've found that people often make errors when using this approach – errors that result in data loss and data duplication – so I won't be covering the merge function here.

Throughout the spreadsheet, avoid spaces and any special characters (e.g., $ or \) since they mean different things in R than they probably mean to you. If they're there and you don't need to analyze anything from those columns, that's fine – just leave them alone. But if you want to use data from the column, you need to convert them. To do this, you can create a new column that includes R-friendly input but that codes the same info as in your original column. Instead of spaces, you can use a full stop/period or a capital letter to separate words in a cell: subj.number or SubjNumber is fine. Whatever you do, be consistent across your spreadsheet so that you don't need to consult your spreadsheet every time you want to type a command in R. (I like to use all lower case in the headers of my spreadsheets for this reason.)

When naming the spreadsheet and any folders that the spreadsheet is in, separate with a dash (i.e., -) if you need to separate words. I like to use short names that are distinct across my various studies.

Some other advice:

- Don't leave any column names blank.
- Don't name two columns the same thing, even if they contain the exact same information.

- Don't leave cells blank and don't write NA in any cell. Leaving them blank or writing NA won't break R, but it's easier to subset those rows out if they contain something else.

- Don't use letters or other characters in a column for a numeric factor.

- Don't use only numbers in a column for a discrete factor.

- Don't start a column name with a number. (Use cool.factor1 instead of 1cool.factor.)

- R can be run in some languages other than English and you can use other languages in the console. More information can be found at: https://cran.r-project.org/bin/windows/base/rw-FAQ. html#I-want-to-run-R-in-Chinese_002fJapanese_002fKorean.

- There are ways to import your data from other statistical systems (e.g., SPSS). You can find more information here: https://cran.r-project.org/doc/manuals/r-release/R-data.html#EpiInfo-Minitab-SAS-S_002dPLUS-SPSS-Stata-Systat.

- Save a copy of the spreadsheet as a.csv file

Note that none of the formatting in your spreadsheet (e.g., highlights) will be maintained in the csv file. So if you have, say, all tokens that are preceded by a bilabial coded in green, that should instead be coded in its own column. R is quite happy with lots and lots of columns and rows, so don't hold back on R's account. In fact, not holding back on the number of rows and columns goes for all kinds of stuff; if responses are similar in a way that you might want to bundle them up and treat them as the same for analysis, then create a new column and code it that way before you begin running stats, but leave the original column there, too, so you have a record of your work. Doing any bundling prior to analysis is a good idea for two reasons: (1) it will make your life easier with less R code and a more easily retrievable analysis, and (2) it will avoid biasing your statistical analysis toward something that wasn't even a part of your hypothesis. When saving your spreadsheet, you'll need to decide on a format. R can't read all formats, so you need to select one that you can use with R. My preference is to have a master spreadsheet (saved as .xlsx) that contains notes, a filter function, and multiple sheets, and then to use this master spreadsheet to create single sheet csv files to be read into R. When saving to csv format, take care that your data are coded as specified in this chapter so that you don't experience data loss.

Don't worry: these "rules" become second nature and you'll soon be setting up R-friendly spreadsheets for your data without even thinking about it.

6.1.2. Getting started

Now comes the fun bit. If you haven't done it already, you'll need to install R. The version I'm working with for this chapter is R version 3.2.4. It's also a great idea to install RStudio, which helps make R a little more user friendly.

Before you begin, you need to make sure you set your working directory to the folder on your computer that contains the spreadsheet. You will need to do this every time you start R. One option is to use the drop-down menu to select your working directory. (If using R Studio: Session → Set Working Directory → Choose Directory…) Alternatively, you can use the command line option, where you can specify the folder location in between the quote marks.

```
setwd("~/Desktop/Work/methods-book")
```

You will need to specify the directory anytime you open R and anytime you've previously specified a different directory. (You can't specify multiple directories in the same session. However, you can toggle between different scripts in R Studio, running analyses of different datasets that have already been loaded into R.)

Once you've set the directory, you should read your spreadsheet in to R. To illustrate the code for this, I'll be using the sample spreadsheet, my.amazing.data.csv, which is available on the companion website. The spreadsheet contains fake data. If you get an error message when trying to read in the data, check that the csv spreadsheet name matches the name of the csv file in the script. If it still doesn't work, check that you've specified the working directory and that you've saved the spreadsheet in the folder that you specified as the working directory.

```
my.amazing.data <- read.csv("my-amazing-data.csv", T)
```

The syntax used for reading data into R is very typical, so it's worth spending some time understanding how to interpret it. On the right hand side is the command (read.csv) with details about what the command should address within the parentheses. Thus, we are asking R to read a csv file, and then we provide the name of the file we want to read in to R (my-amazing-data.csv), followed by a comma and a <T> to indicate that the spreadsheet has headers (i.e., headers = TRUE). Then, we specify how we want to refer to this particular dataset in R (my.amazing.data) by placing the name left of the arrow. Note that I've uses dashes in the name of the csv file and periods in the name given to the dataset in R.

For the remainder of this chapter, I won't step through the meaning of each component in this much detail. The best way for you to learn it is to try substituting text in for the different parts so that you can find out what they mean on your own.

My spreadsheet has columns for two sample dependent variables (DVs): my.DV1 (which represents a continuous variable) and my.DV2 (which represents a discrete variable). There are also columns for two predicting variables that are numeric (cool.factor1 and cool.factor2) and two that are discrete (cool.factor3 and cool.factor4). In the example code given in this chapter, I will use the name and header labels from the spreadsheet. Be sure to replace them with the headers you've used in your own dataset once you start working with your own data.

To make sure that R read in all the data correctly, it's a good idea to request a summary:

```
summary(my.amazing.data)
```

To check specific columns, specify the column name after $:

```
summary(my.amazing.data$subject)
summary(my.amazing.data$my.DV1)
```

Check that you don't have any empty cells; for these, R provides a number with no level label. Also check that the entries are what you believe them to be and that R is treating each level appropriately. For example, since R is case sensitive, it might have identified more categories than you intend there to be (e.g., 'Happy', 'happy', 'Joy', and 'joy', when 'Happy' and 'happy' are intended to be one category, and 'Joy' and 'joy' are intended to be another). The easiest way to fix those sorts of errors is to fix them in your spreadsheet and read the data back in.

Depending on how you've labeled your factor levels, you might find that something that is meant to be discrete is getting treated as continuous (where the R summary gives you a min and max value), or vice versa (where the R summary provides the number of times each value appears). This will happen if you've coded a discrete factor using numbers (e.g., 1 and 0) or a continuous factor with a letter anywhere in the column (e.g., either 1a, 1b, 1c or 1, 2, 3, na). That's not a problem with the sample spreadsheet, but here's the syntax just in case.

```
my.amazing.data$subject
    <- as.factor(my.amazing.data$subject)
```

The code for converting from a discrete factor to a numeric one is similar, but it can produce problematic values. Thus, I recommend setting up your spreadsheet in a way where R automatically reads it as numeric. In other words, make sure there is no non-numeric text in a column that is intended to be numeric.

Any changes like this that you make in R will need to be made every time that you reload the data into R. Because of this, I usually set aside part of my R script where I copy and paste all of the load commands, labeled with something obvious (e.g., ##***LOAD DATA HERE!!***##) that is easily findable using RStudio's search function. For notes like this, use a hashtag anywhere in the line prior to the note to comment it out so R won't mistake it for code that should be run.

Another function that you will find useful is the subsetting function. Let's say I only want to consider responses when cool.factor3 is equal to YES. I would use the following:

```
YES.to.3 <-
my.amazing.data[my.amazing.data$cool.factor3 == "YES",]
```

Try running different summaries over this subset of the data to get a better sense of what this code does. Also, try calling a variety of contingency tables to get an idea of how the factors in the dataset are related to one another.

```
xtabs(~my.DV2+cool.factor4,YES.to.3)
```

Then, you can create a shortcut that will mean you don't have to specify my.amazing.data$ in every single line and instead you'll be able to just use the column names. To do this, use:

```
attach(my.amazing.data)
```

However, if you are working simultaneously with different datasets that contain identical column names, it's best that you do not use the attach() function so that you don't accidentally analyze the wrong thing.

6.2. Creating plots and graphs

Graphs can be generated using the built-in R libraries or using one of the add-on libraries, such as ggplot2. The built-in options are generally faster and simpler, which means they're a great way to visualize your data quickly and, in some cases, they make excellent publishable graphs. However, if you want more control over how the graph looks, then ggplot2 is the way to go. In this section, I'll present code for creating graphs using the built-in libraries, plus a couple of non-standard options that are gaining in popularity. Thus, I will be using ggplot minimally, but if you are interested in learning ggplot2, check out Cookbook for R: http://www.cookbook-r.com/Graphs/. In addition to presenting code for plotting raw data, I explain how to produce plots using the models' predictions after discussing regression models in Section 6.6.

In the following sections, I present when to use each type of graph and I provide the code you can use to plot it. These sections cover scatterplots (Section 6.2.1), density plots (Section 6.2.2), line graphs (Section 6.2.3), bar plots and histograms (Section 6.2.4), box and whisker plots (Section 6.2.5), and bean plots (Section 6.2.6). While the graphs are shown in grey-scale in the text, I've used colors in the code for demonstration purposes. The original graphs are available in color on the companion website.

When to use what?

Scatterplots: use when comparing two factors, both of which are continuous and are hypothesized to be correlated, or if you want to demonstrate that there is no correlation between the two factors.

Density plots: use to visualize distributions of a continuous variable. Can be used to examine relationships between a continuous variable and an ordered, discrete, or continuous variable.

Line graphs: use when comparing counts or percentages of responses to levels of an ordered factor, or when the dependent variable is continuous and the independent variable is ordered.

Bar plots: use when wanting to visualize counts for one or more discrete factors. When plotting a numeric dependent variable, boxplots or beanplots are generally more powerful visualization tools.

Histograms: use when showing counts for an ordered DV. If examining effects of an IV with more than two factor levels, use a line graph instead.

Box plots: use when the DV is continuous and you have one predicting factor that is discrete or an interaction between two factors that are discrete.

Bean plots: use when the DV is continuous and you have one predicting factor that is discrete or an interaction between two factors that are discrete. This option is increasingly preferred over bar graphs and boxplots because the visualization of spread is clearer, and it is especially clear when there is an interaction.

6.2.1. Scatterplots

Scatterplots are plots of two continuous variables (e.g., formant values, reaction times, or ratings from a task that uses a VAS). They are very useful to demonstrate a correlation between the variables, or a lack thereof.

Figure 6.1   Sample scatterplot based on my amazing (and fake) data

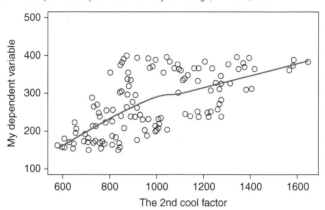

They can also be used to show distributions. To generate a scatterplot, you can use the following code:

```
plot(cool.factor2, my.DV1, ylim=(c(100,500)),
    xlab="The 2nd cool factor",

    ylab="my dependent variable")
```

If you'd like to add a curved line through the center of the distribution, you can use lines (lowess) after creating the plot.

```
lines(lowess(cool.factor2, my.DV1), col="blue")
```

The resulting graph is shown in Figure 6.1.

Scatterplots are a great way to visualize comparisons between two continuous variables. Thus, they are often used by sociolinguists and phoneticians to plot vowel formants. To do this in R, you need to specify the different vowels or environments being tested separately. From our sample spreadsheet, let's pretend that cool.factor2 is a column of F2 measurements and my.DV1 is a column of F1 measurements. Also, let's pretend that when cool.factor4 equals HIGH, it's referring to tokens that are pre-lateral and when it is equal to LOW it's all other environments. To plot this, I could use:

```
plot(my.amazing.data$cool.factor2,
my.amazing.data$my.DV1,
    xlim=c(1800, 500), ylim=c(500,90),
    xlab="F2 (Normalized)", ylab="F1 (Normalized)",
    type="n", main="Vowel plot as a scatterplot")
points(
```

```
    my.amazing.data[my.amazing.data$cool.
factor4=="HIGH",]
    $cool.factor2, my.amazing.data[my.amazing.
data$cool.factor4=="HIGH",]
    $my.DV1,
    pch=1, col="purple")
points(
    my.amazing.data[my.amazing.data$cool.
factor4=="LOW",]
    $cool.factor2,
    my.amazing.data[my.amazing.data$cool.
factor4=="LOW",]
    $my.DV1,
    pch=2, col="lightblue")
```

The resulting graph is shown in Figure 6.2. Note that I've specified the values for the x- and y-axes using xlim=c(), ylim=c(). This allows me to reverse the axes so that the plot looks like a vowel plot; R will automatically update the placement of the points accordingly. When working with your own data, you'll need to re-specify these values depending on the minimum and maximum values you observe for F1 and F2. Also note that in this plot() section, I've used type="n". This tells R to create the plot as specified but not to plot the points just yet. Then, we can add the specific points we want, first for those when cool.factor4=HIGH and then for those where is in coded as LOW, selecting my choice of colors (col= "insert a color name") and shape (pch=insert a number).

The code provided to produce Figure 6.2 is helpful when plotting many different vowels. A simpler option when working with only two vowels (or two factors influencing the realization of a single vowel), is to use ifelse,

Figure 6.2   Sample scatterplot of vowel formants

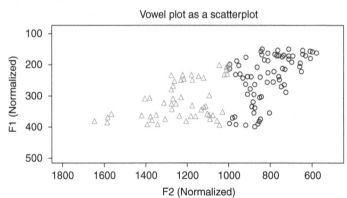

which tells R to use option 1 (here=purple) if the specified condition is met and to use option 1 (here=lightblue) otherwise.

```
plot(my.amazing.data$cool.factor2,
     my.amazing.data$my.DV1,
     xlim=c(1800, 500), ylim=c(500,90),
     xlab="F2 (Normalized)", ylab="F1 (Normalized)",
     col=ifelse(((cool.factor4=="HIGH")),"purple",
     "lightblue"),
     pch=ifelse(((cool.factor4=="HIGH")), 17, 1),
     main="Vowel plot"
)
```

And yet another option is to use the vowelplot() function from the vowels library. However, this requires using a specific setup for the spreadsheet, so most people I work with tend to prefer other options.

6.2.2. Density plots

Density plots are commonly used to check whether the data are normally distributed and whether there is skew in the distribution. This is important to know so that, when you're deciding on the best statistical test for your data, you can choose between using a parametric test (which assumes that data are normally distributed) or nonparametric test (which doesn't make this assumption). To examine the distribution, you would use a simple density plot, such as that in Figure 6.3, which shows the bell shaped curve associated with a normal distribution.

Figure 6.3   Graph showing what a normal distribution looks like

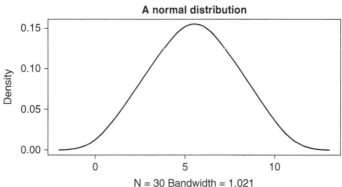

Figure 6.4   A density plot of a dependent variable showing a bimodal (i.e., not a normal) distribution

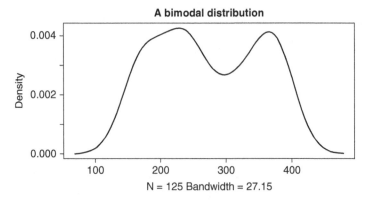

Figure 6.5   A plot showing the density of the dependent variable across two levels of a discrete factor

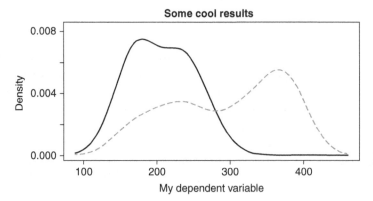

For practice, let's try this with the fake data in the sample spreadsheet. Specifically, let's say we want to know whether the distribution of my.DV1 is normally distributed. To test this, I would use:

```
sample.density <- density(my.amazing.data$my.DV1)
plot(sample.density, main="A bimodal distribution")
```

The output is shown in Figure 6.4. This graph shows two bumps rather than the one bell shape shown in Figure 6.3. In some cases, the two bumps can be the cause of some underlying factor, such as Condition.

Using density plots to visualize your data can also be helpful in other ways as well. For instance, you might want to compare the distributions of a dependent variable across different predicting factors, as shown in Figure 6.5.

To do this, I installed the sm package:

```
install.packages("sm")
```

And loaded it:

```
library(sm)
```

And then used the following R syntax:

```
attach(my.amazing.data)
sm.density.compare(my.DV1, cool.factor3, xlab="my
    dependent variable")
title(main="Some cool results")
```

Any time you install a new package, R will download a bunch of stuff and you'll watch everything zip by as this happens. Don't be alarmed by this; it's exactly what this command is supposed to do. Luckily, you only need to install each package once, not every time you load the data into R.

Some sociolinguists (e.g., Grama 2015) have used ggplot to create density plots for formant values, as shown in Figure 6.6. The most central blob within each distribution indicates the densest portion of the distribution (i.e., that's where the tokens are most-heavily clustered).

To create this plot, you need to install and load ggplot. (Try figuring out how to do this by consulting the R syntax used for the sm package. Then have a look at the sample R script to check your work.)

Figure 6.6   Sample of a vowel plot shown as a density plot

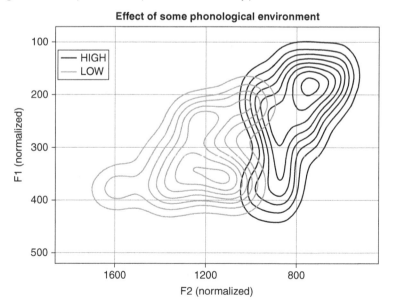

```
ggplot(my.amazing.data,
     aes(x = cool.factor2, y = my.DV1,
     color=factor(cool.factor4))) +
     geom_density2d(aes(label= factor(cool.factor4))) +
     xlim(1800, 500) + ylim(500, 90) +
     theme_bw() +
     ggtitle("Effect of some phonological environment") +
     ylab("F1 (normalized)") + xlab("F2 (normalized)") +
     scale_colour_manual("",
     breaks = c("HIGH", "LOW"),
     values = c("purple", "lightblue"))
```

Compared to using scatterplots to plot formant values, I find these types of plots to be particularly helpful when visualizing data from especially large datasets when density in a scatterplot is unclear due to a large number of overlapping tokens (i.e., not with the sample dataset).

6.2.3. Line graphs

Line graphs can be used when the dependent variable is an ordered variable, or when the dependent variable is discrete but the independent variable is ordered. (You may remember from Section 2.1.2, ordered factors are those that have a clear order but are really categories rather than continuous variables (e.g., age groups, levels of language endangerment, or responses on a rating task), whereas discrete variables are those that are non-ordered categories (e.g., quotative verb produced).) In both cases, the dependent variable is graphed as counts, percentages, or proportions.

Line graphs can also be used when the dependent variable is continuous (e.g., vowel duration) and the independent variable is ordered (e.g., four categories of vowel height). In this case, the dependent variable is plotted on the y-axis and the ordered independent variable is plotted on the x-axis.

To create a line graph showing percentages of cool.factor1=YES responses, I need a vector of the percentages. But before I can do that I need to calculate those percentages.

I can view the distribution of the data using a cross tabulation/contingency table.

```
xtabs(~cool.factor1+cool.factor4,my.amazing.data)
```

And then I can use these values to calculate percentages. For each percentage, I'm going to create a new object.

```
H3 <- 5/(6)*100
H4 <- 8/(10)*100
H5 <- 6/(10)*100
H6 <- 10/(12)*100
H7 <- 12/(17)*100
H8 <- 8/(34)*100
H9 <- 11/(16)*100
H10 <- 8/(18)*100
```

And then I use these objects to create a vector.

```
High <- c(100, H3, H4, H5, H6, H7, H8, H9, H10)
```

And then I use this vector to create the plot.

```
plot(High, ylab="Percentage of HIGH responses",
     xlab="The 1st cool factor")
lines(High, type = "o", col = "blue")
```

The resulting graph is shown in Figure 6.7.

Line graphs can also be created in ggplot, which I find to be simpler even though there's a bit of a learning curve with ggplot. If you've already worked through the section on density plots, you've already installed ggplot and there's no need to do it again. However, if you skipped that section, then you'll need to install the package:

```
install.packages("ggplot")
```

And then load your new library using:

```
library(ggplot2)
```

Now, we're ready to plot the data. I want to plot the effect of conditions (HIGH and LOW in my.DV2).

Figure 6.7   Sample line graph using vectors to plot a percent

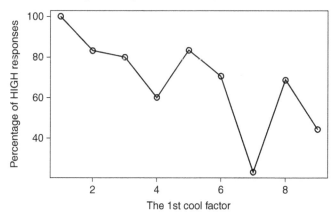

Figure 6.8 Sample line graph created using ggplot

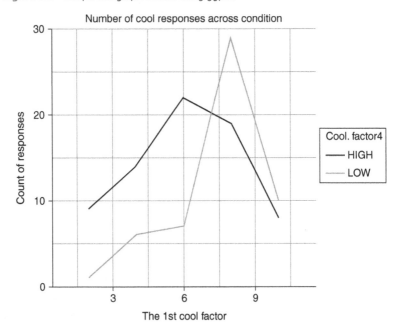

```
ggplot(data=my.amazing.data,
    aes(x=cool.factor1, group=cool.factor4,
    colour=cool.factor4)) +
    geom_line(aes(fill=..count..), stat="bin",
    binwidth=2) +
    xlab("The 1st cool factor") + ylab("Count of
    responses") +
    ggtitle("Number of cool responses across
    condition") +
    guides(fill=FALSE)
```

The resulting graph is shown in Figure 6.8.

Please see the R Cookbook for instructions on how to edit your plots created in the program to make them even more beautiful.

6.2.4. Bar plots and histograms

Bar plots can be used to show counts of a discrete factor or show the relationship between two or more discrete factors. Bar plots are increasingly used only for data exploration rather than the final data visualization that

Figure 6.9   Sample bar plot

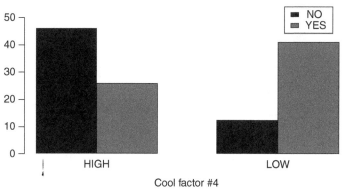

Figure 6.10   Sample histogram

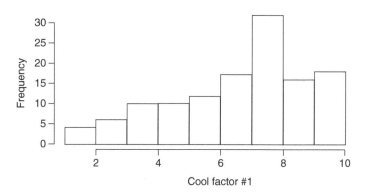

would be used in a paper or presentation, so I won't dedicate too much space to them here.

```
counts <- table(my.amazing.data$my.DV2,
    my.amazing.data$cool.factor4)
    barplot(counts, main="Car Distribution",
    xlab="Number of Gears", ylim=(c(0,55)),
    col=c("darkblue","red"),
    legend = rownames(counts), beside=TRUE)
```

The resulting graph is shown in Figure 6.9.

Histograms are a lot like bar plots that show counts of a factor. However, the dependent variable must be ordered and, in R, treated as numeric. Therefore, for the example, we'll use the ordered factor cool.factor1.

```
hist(my.amazing.data$cool.factor1,
    xlab="Cool factor #1", main="I am a histogram")
```

6.2.5. Box and whisker plots

Box and whisker plots can be used to demonstrate a relationship between one continuous variable and one or more discrete variables. They can also be used when all of the variables are discrete if the dependent variable is converted to a percentage.

In a box plot, the box represents the two middle quartiles, with the median marked as a line somewhere within the box. Whiskers are used to indicate the outer two quartiles of the data, and outliers are shown as dots.

```
boxplot(my.DV1 ~ cool.factor3*cool.factor4,
    data=my.amazing.data,
    main="I am a boxplot",
    ylab="my dependent variable")
```

The resulting plot is shown in Figure 6.11.

6.2.6. Bean plots

Bean plots are not commonly used, but they're a great visualization tool. They're like a box and whiskers plot in that spread is shown, but (as shown in Figure 6.12) they're presented as a density plot along the y-axis, which means the reader gets more information about the distribution of

Figure 6.11   Sample boxplot

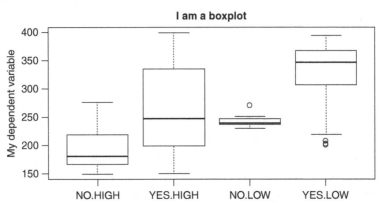

the data. They take a little getting used to at first since most people aren't accustomed to visualizing data in this way, but they're so useful that – once you get used to them – you'll probably become obsessed and want to use them for everything.

To create a bean plot, install and load the beanplot package.

```
install.packages("beanplot")
require(beanplot)
```

Then plot the data using code such as this:

```
beanplot(my.DV1 ~ cool.factor3*cool.factor4,
    data=my.amazing.data, ll = 0.03,
    main = "Cool Interaction", side = "both",
xlab=" Cool factor #3", ylab="My dependent variable",
col = list("purple", c("lightblue", "black")),
axes=F)axis(1, at=c(1, 2), labels=c("NO", "YES"))
    axis(2)
legend("topleft", fill = c("purple", "lightblue"),
    legend = c("HIGH", "LOW"), box.lty=0)
```

The default in the bean plot package is for the heavy horizontal black line to represent the mean. However, this can be switched to the median, as in:

Figure 6.12   An example of a bean plot, showing an interaction between two predicting variables

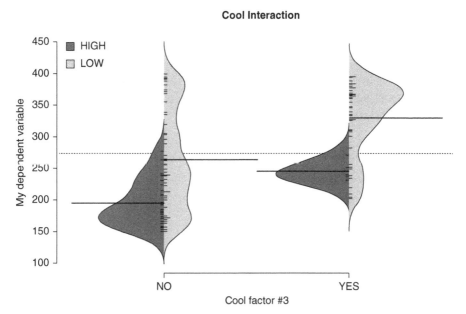

```
beanplot(my.DV1 ~ cool.factor3*cool.factor4,
    data=my.amazing.data, ll = 0.03,
    main = "Cool Interaction", side = "both", xlab="
    Cool factor #3", ylab="My dependent variable",
    col = list("purple", c("lightblue", "black")),
    axes=F, overallline = "median")
    axis(1, at=c(1, 2), labels=c("NO", "YES"))
    axis(2)
legend("topleft", fill = c("purple", "lightblue"),
    legend = c("HIGH", "LOW"), box.lty=0)
```

If you are looking for ways to plot multiple graphs side-by-side or a way to save a plot as a high resolution image (the default in R is annoyingly low), I've included some of the code at the beginning of the section on graphs in the example R script (script-to-analyze-my-amazing-data.R). Enjoy!

6.3. Preparing to conduct statistical analysis

Before beginning any statistical analysis, it's important to know about the nature of the data. To do this, consider what types of variables you have and plot your data in several different ways.

It's also important to make sure the levels of your factors are treated in a way that make them the most interpretable. This means that, sometimes, you will need to change which level R is treating as a baseline. If you have a control condition, the control is normally your baseline, so that the test conditions are compared to the control. If you do not have a control condition, you should change the baseline to whichever level helps make the results more interpretable. To change the baseline, we use the relevel function:

```
my.amazing.data$new.factor4 <-
    relevel(my.amazing.data$cool.factor4, re="LOW")
```

When you compare summaries of the two factors, you'll see that the order in which the levels are shown has reversed, indicating the baseline has changed.

```
> summary(my.amazing.data$cool.factor4)
HIGH  LOW
  72   53
> summary(my.amazing.data$new.factor4)
  LOW  HIGH
  53   72
```

For numeric variables, it is recommended that the variable be scaled to its mean so that the intercept value can be interpreted as the estimated value for the dependent variable when the numeric predicting variables are at their mean value. This is especially recommended if the minimum value of the numeric variable isn't zero and you're using a regression model. To rescale a numeric factor, you can use:

```
my.amazing.data$cool2.rescaled <-
    scale(my.amazing.data$cool.factor2, center=T,
    scale=T)
```

Failing to rescale to the mean does not affect the direction of an effect of a variable or level of significance reported in a model's output, but it does affect how you interpret the exact value of an intercept.

For statistical analysis, outliers can be a problem. These can come in the form of a participant, a token, or a single stimulus item that behaves differently from the others. One reason they're important to remove prior to statistical analysis is that they can bias the analysis, making it appear as though there is some trend that's not really there or else hide a trend that would otherwise be there.

Tokens can become outliers when participants fail to attend to a stimulus; a failure to attend can occur as a result of fatigue, equipment failure, or a distraction in the environment. Stimulus items can become outliers if the participants perceive them differently from the other stimuli for some reason. For example, an item might induce different behavior than other items if it has more background noise, is perceived as less natural, or is more likely to draw attention due to, for example, amplitude or color brightness. Participants can become outliers when they do not or cannot behave like they normally would. This can result from a range of factors, including equipment failure, language proficiency, poor vision or hearing, feelings of stress, or being under the influence of drugs or alcohol. In addition, some participants don't take their role as a research subject seriously, employing tactics such as responding to every question on a forced-choice task with the first option in an attempt to advance through the experiment more quickly and with the least effort. Non-serious participants can be identified both by their outlier status and their responses to the "safeguard" questions discussed in Section 2.1.3. However, as sociolinguists, the last thing we want to do is outright discard data from a participant who is an outlier in the data. This is because – sometimes – participants are outliers because they're doing something interesting. Such cases may warrant special treatment and consideration. Since it is often difficult in experimental work to differentiate these participants from those who are outliers for uninteresting reasons, all outliers are usually removed.

6.4. An introduction to statistical methods

There are a wide variety of statistical tests that you can use, and covering them all is well beyond the scope of this book. Therefore, I focus here on some of the most commonly used ones, describing when to use them and providing the R code used to run them.

When to use what?

Each of the tests in Section 6.4 assume independence of observations, meaning that if you have multiple responses or tokens from a single participant, none of these tests is right for you. Go instead to Section 6.5.

Correlations: use when you want to see whether there is a significant relationship between two and only two factors, and those factors are numbers.

Wilcoxon Rank Sum (i.e., Mann-Whitney test): use when you have a numeric response that you are comparing across groups that are made up of different individuals.

Wilcoxon Signed Rank Test: use when you have a numeric response that you are comparing across groups when the participants in both groups are the same.

Chi-squared: use when you have a single categorical response that you are comparing across two groups, and you want to test whether the two groups are significantly different.

Fisher's Exact: use when you have data that would be appropriate for a chi-squared but your dataset is small and/or you have fewer than five responses in any given cell.

See Section 2.1.2 for a discussion of the different types of variables, with examples.

6.4.1. Correlations

Researchers test for a correlation when they have two and only two numeric variables, and they are normally plotted using a scatterplot. (I'm focusing here on biserial correlations rather than point biserial ones due to frequency of use in sociolinguistics.) For example, I might want to test the relationship between a participant's age and their mean response time. I would first produce a scatterplot, with age on the x-axis and response time on the y-axis, and then I could test for a correlation using one of the correlation tests described in this section.

These tests assume independence of observations, so you should not use a correlation test when the two variables are dependent on one another, or when responses within one of the variables are dependent on another. For example, these types of tests would be inappropriate when analyzing the effect of Condition on a dependent variable if each participant provided more than one response. Instead, linear regression should be used, or related values (e.g., all of those provided by a participant) should be collated (e.g., as a mean) prior to running the correlation test.

There are three types of correlation tests: Pearson's *r* correlation, Spearman rank correlation, and Kendall's tau. Below, I outline the main differences between them to help you identify which one is most appropriate for your purposes. Note that while I've provided R code for running these tests over the sample spreadsheet, we violate the assumption of independence of observations since we have multiple responses from individual participants. Therefore, let's pretend for the purposes of this exercise that every row corresponds to a response from a unique participant.

Pearson's *r* correlation

- must be continuous, not ordered
- is parametric: both variables should be normally distributed
- is used with large datasets

Pearson is the default correlation method used by R, so no method needs to be specified. Thus, to run a Pearson's correlation use:

```
cor.test(my.amazing.data$my.DV1,
    my.amazing.data$cool.factor1)
```

Spearman's ρ (rho) rank correlation

- can be ordinal or continuous
- is non-parametric
- is used with large datasets

In contrast, when running a Spearman rank correlation test, the method must be specified:

```
cor.test(my.amazing.data$my.DV1,
    my.amazing.data$cool.factor1, method="spearm")
```

Kendall's tau (τ) rank correlation

- can be ordinal or continuous
- is non-parametric
- is used with relatively small datasets

To run a Kendall's rank correlation test, use:

```
cor.test(my.amazing.data$my.DV1,
    my.amazing.data$cool.factor1, method="kendall")
```

Regardless of the type of correlation test used, a positive number for the output (the correlation coefficient not the *p*-value) indicates a positive correlation whereas a negative number indicates a negative correlation.

6.4.2. Wilcoxon Rank Sum and Wilcoxon Signed Rank Test

Like correlation tests, the Wilcoxon Rank Sum (also known as a Mann-Whitney test, a two-sample test, and an unpaired Wilcoxon) and Signed Rank Tests (also known as a one-sample test and as a paired Wilcoxon) are used with numeric data. However, Wilcoxon tests are used to test whether the two factors are significantly different rather than if they're significantly correlated.

Which of the two types of Wilcoxon tests you should use depends on whether the data from the two groups come from the same participants or not: if so, use the Signed Rank Test (where responses are "paired" across the groups) and, if not, use the Rank Sum test (where responses are "unpaired"). For example, if you are testing whether there is a significant difference between self-determined rating of their comprehension of a dialect for participants from region A versus participants from region B, then you should use the Mann-Whitney test. If instead you're testing whether the same participant shifts in their rating depending on, say, exposure to a social prime, you would use a Wilcoxon Signed Rank Test.

Do not use either of these tests when you have responses that are not independent from one another. Thus, this should not be used when analyzing multiple responses from a single individual, such as when analyzing the primary data from a matched-guise rating task where participants respond to multiple tokens.

In order to use our sample spreadsheet to demonstrate these tests, I'm afraid we once again have to pretend like each row in the example spreadsheet comes from a separate participant.

For a two-sample test, use a Wilcoxon Rank Sum test, as in:

```
wilcox.test(my.amazing.data$cool.factor1, cool.factor2)
```

For a one-sample test, specify that responses across groups are matched by participant by adding paired=TRUE:

```
wilcox.test(my.amazing.data$cool.factor1, cool.factor2,
  paired=TRUE)
```

6.4.3. Chi-squared

While correlations are used to determine whether two distributions are significantly related, chi-squared (like the two Wilcoxon tests) is used to determine whether behavior across the two groups is significantly different. They are most appropriate in cases when there is a single categorical response across two (or more) groups. For example, chi-squared might be used when testing whether there is a significant difference between people from rural versus urban areas in whether they ever produce double modal constructions (e.g., *might could*).

Chi-squared should **not be used** when responses are not independent from one another. Thus, you should not use a chi-squared when you have multiple responses from a single individual, like the primary data collected using most experimental designs. A chi-squared should also not be used if responses across the two groups aren't mutually exclusive.

As with the correlation and Wilcoxon tests, the sample spreadsheet isn't really set up appropriately for chi-squared since it includes multiple responses from a single participant. However, we can use it to demonstrate a chi-squared test for the purposes of learning how to do it as long as we pretend like each row corresponds to a response from a different participant. (Just like we did when we were running correlation tests and Wilcoxons.)

```
chisq.test(my.amazing.data$cool.factor3,
    my.amazing.data$cool.factor4)
```

But before you run a chi-squared test, create a contingency table using the factors you plan to test using the chi-squared. Chi-squared requires that you have at least five responses in each of the cells in the table. If you have fewer than five responses in any given cell, you should use a different test, such as Fisher's Exact.

6.4.4. Fisher's Exact

A Fisher's Exact test is used instead of chi-squared when working with a small dataset. To run a Fisher's Exact test, you would use:

```
fisher.test(my.amazing.data$cool.factor3,
  my.amazing.data$cool.factor4)
```

Please note that, like chi-squared, Fisher's Exact assumes independence of observations.

6.5. Mixed effects models

Currently, the preferred statistical method for analyzing experimental sociolinguistic data is the use of multivariate regression models with random effects. These types of models are often referred to colloquially as mixed effects models since they use both fixed effects (which are made up of the usual dependent variables) and random effects (factors sampled from a limited set). Participants and items are commonly treated as random effects in the experimental sociolinguistics literature. The effects are called random because the model assigns a coefficient to each factor level, allowing each level to vary randomly from the model's predicted intercept. To understand what this means, it helps to know something about how regression works. All regression models consider the input data and "draw" a line that approximates the best fit through the data. For linear regression, you can picture a scatterplot with a straight line that tries to go through all of the data points without bending. For logistic regression, the model converts the discrete values to numbers (log odds), which it then attempts to fit a line through in the same way as with linear regression. In both cases, the line intersects the y-axis at some point and it has a certain slope associated with it. The point where the line intersects the y-axis is known as the intercept. In the simplest of mixed effects models, it is the intercept that varies across the different levels of the random factor, so, for example, different participants are assigned different intercept values. Random slopes can also be added. These assign a different value for the slope of the line (as opposed to the intercept) so that, for example, participants can vary in the extent to which they're influenced by the independent variables (fixed effects) specified.

Some fun facts about regression models with random intercepts and slopes:

- You can have lots of different predicting factors/independent variables.

- The predicting factors can be continuous or ordinal or discrete.
- You can examine the main effects and interactions that a factor is involved in, in the same model.
- Simpler models without random effects can be used instead but most experimental work in sociolinguistics now uses random effects.

There is still quite a bit of disagreement as to whether we should "go maximal" with our random effects structure (with all possible combinations of slopes and intercepts) or whether we should use the simplest model that significantly improves the model's fit. Given how rapidly opinions seem to shift and that this book will not be updated annually, I recommend checking out the latest and greatest arguments for yourself.

Which type of regression model you should use depends on your dependent variable: a linear regression model is used for a continuous variable; a logistic regression model is used for a discrete, binary dependent variable; and an ordinal model is used for an ordered dependent variable. All three of these models are capable of handling a variety of different types of independent variable; when deciding between these three types of regression models, your independent variables have no bearing on determining which one you should use.

Why not Analysis of Variance (ANOVA)?

ANOVA is not commonly used in experimental sociolinguistics because it assumes independence of observations, an assumption which is violated in the data from many experimental paradigms. For example, in the visual world paradigm, behavior in one time window is highly dependent on the adjacent ones, so an ANOVA would be inappropriate. Instead, regression is preferred. When working with data where it's safe to assume independence of observations, tests that are simpler than ANOVA (like chi-squared and t-tests) are generally preferred except in cases when there are multiple independent variables.

When to use what?

Linear regression: use when you want to see whether one or more factors influence the dependent variable and the dependent variable is continuous.

Logistic regression: use when you want to see whether one or more factors influence the dependent variable and the dependent variable is binary

Ordinal regression: use when you want to see whether one or more factors influence the dependent variable and the dependent variable is ordered.

6.5.1. Linear regression with random effects

Linear regression is a commonly used type of model when testing the effect of more than one factor on a continuous variable. For example, they are often used to examine effects of factors influencing reaction times and formant values taken at the target of a vowel.

Linear regression should not be used when analyzing data that is ordinal rather than continuous (e.g., data from a rating task), though it is often used this way. I've run tests comparing linear and ordinal models fit to ordered data in several different datasets of mine and haven't observed any difference in the overall direction or significance levels of the effects tested. That said, linear models are not the best representation of ordinal data, so – if you're working with ordinal data – you might want to go to Section 6.5.3 instead.

To use a linear mixed effects model in R, you first need to install the lme4 package if you haven't done so already:

```
install.packages("lme4")
```

Then you need to load the package:

```
library(lme4)
```

For this example, I'll test a linear mixed effects model with my.DV1 as the dependent variable and three predicting factors: cool.factor1, cool.factor2, and cool.factor3. I'll also include the participant (coded in my spreadsheet as "subject") as a random intercept, which allows the model to take into consideration that not all participants may behave exactly the same way in regard to the dependent variable. For example, subject 1a might have an overall bias in terms of my.DV1 that is not found for subject 2a.

```
my.amazing.model1 <- lmer(my.DV1 ~ cool.factor1 +
  cool.factor2 + cool.factor3 + (1|subject),
  data = my.amazing.data)
```

Then, I use summary to view the model's output:

```
summary(my.amazing.model1)
```

This first model tests for effects of three different factors hypothesized to influence the dependent variable, each as main effects (i.e., no interactions). The second model is a lot like the first except that it includes an interaction between cool.factor2 and cool.factor3, which we specify using an asterisk between the factors instead of a plus sign. It also tests each of the two interacting factors as main effects. The other fixed effect (cool.factor1) is included only as a main effect.

```
my.amazing.model2 <- lmer(my.DV1 ~ cool.factor1 +
  cool.factor2 * cool.factor3 + (1|subject),
  data = my.amazing.data)
  summary(my.amazing.model2)
```

And if I want to include a by-participant random slope for cool.factor1 in addition to a random intercept for participant, I would use:

```
my.amazing.model4 <- lmer(my.DV1 ~ cool.factor1 + (1 +
  cool.factor1|subject),
  data = my.amazing.data)
  summary(my.amazing.model4)
```

If I want to include a by-participant random slope for cool.factor1 but no by-participant intercept, I would remove the "1 +" from where I specify the random effect structure.

```
my.amazing.model4 <- lmer(my.DV1 ~ cool.factor1 +
  (cool.factor1|subject), data = my.amazing.data)
  summary(my.amazing.model4)
```

Take a few minutes to compare each of these models and spot the differences. Then, think about your own data and what factors would be substituted in to each of the spots.

Using a random slope is a good idea if you suspect that different participants might behave differently in the way in which one or more of the factors affect their behavior in regard to the dependent variable. For example, in addition to having an overall bias with regard to my.DV1, the bias may be especially strong when cool.factor3 = YES. To apply this to your own data, think about which of the independent variables that differ across items or participants might have an effect on the dependent variable that varies to some degree across items or participants.

Interpreting the output of a linear regression model

The output from these models is a little more complicated than for the statistical tests we've been working with so far. An annotated example is shown in Figure 6.13.

You may have noticed that the output generated from the models we've produced so far don't report p-values. What gives? Compared to the p-value, the t value is, many say, a more appropriate method for determining the significance of an effect for these types of models. In the social sciences, values of -2 and 2 are generally viewed as the cutoff, just like

Figure 6.13   An annotated example of output from a linear regression model

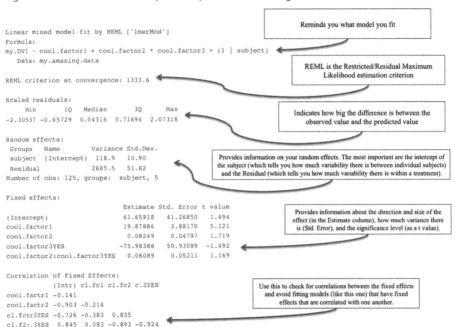

$p<.05$. However, many journals and readers still expect to see p-values, so how do you get them?

There are a few different options though the simplest is to load the lmerTest package. Note that you'll need to install it if you haven't already. After loading the package, re-run your lmer models and voilà!

Also, if you want to calculate the p-value for an interaction, you can run an ANOVA over the model:

```
model.with.interaction <- lmer(my.DV1 ~
   cool.factor1 * cool.factor2 + (1|subject),
   data = my.amazing.data)
anova(model.with.interaction)
```

Plotting effects within the context of a linear mixed effects model

You may have noticed that authors sometimes report graphs of their results within the context of the models rather than graphs based on raw data. The benefit of this is that it allows you to visualize an effect within the context of the other effects included in the model. However, you (as the author) should be sure to also graph your raw data so that you can be sure that you fit an appropriate model and that the graph based on the model's estimated intercepts and coefficients makes sense.

For producing graphs within the context of our model, we'll be using the languageR package.

```
install.packages("languageR")
library(languageR)
```

The syntax you'll use to produce graphs will depend on the nature of the variables included in your model and how many of the independent variables you'd like to include in a single plot. When you want to plot only one continuous predicting factor, use:

```
plotLMER.fnc(my.amazing.model1, pred="cool.factor2",
    xlabel="Cool Factor #2",
    ylabel="Predicted value for my dependent variable")
```

When there are two independent variables and one is numeric and the other is discrete (here, a binary distinction between YES and NO), use:

```
plotLMER.fnc(my.amazing.model2, pred="cool.factor2",
    intr=list("cool.factor3", c("NO", "YES"),
    "end", list(c("lightblue", "purple"), c(1,2))),
    cex=1.0, xlabel="Cool Factor #2", addlines=TRUE,
    ylabel="Predicted value for my dependent variable")
```

When there are two independent variables and both are numeric, use:

```
plotLMER.fnc(my.amazing.model2, pred="cool.factor2",
    intr=list("cool.factor3", c("NO", "YES"),
    "end", list(c("lightblue", "purple"), c(1,2))),
    cex=1.0, xlabel="Cool Factor #2", addlines=TRUE,
    ylabel="Predicted value for my dependent variable")
```

Unfortunately, R syntax sometimes changes across different version of R. Usually this leads to a whole bunch of scholars posting on online discussion forums until someone with more advanced R skills posts a fix. Luckily, this means you can usually find the information you need online. If that information takes a while to come by, you can install an older version of R that still works with the code you need and, since you can have multiple versions of R running on a single computer, you can do this without having to remove the most current version. (However, working outside of R Studio at that point is probably easiest.)

Checking for improvement of model fit

You may have noticed that some authors report that they used an ANOVA to compare two models and, based on the ANOVA's output, they rejected one of the models. This can be a good idea because we often want to use the simplest model that accounts for the most variation in our data. The job of the ANOVA is to compare the two models and determine whether the more complicated one is justified. The more justified it is, the smaller the *p*-value in the ANOVA's output. Before comparing models, you should convert the estimator to a likelihood instead of the Restricted/Residual Maximum Likelihood (REML) estimation criterion. (Translation: rerun the models with REML = FALSE stuck in at the end before you use an ANOVA to compare the models.) This is especially important when you're comparing models that differ in their fixed effects or if you're comparing a model that has random effects to one without.

To run the ANOVA, use:

```
my.amazing.model1 <- lmer(my.DV1 ~ cool.factor1 +
    cool.factor2 +
    cool.factor3 + (1|subject),
    data = my.amazing.data, REML=FALSE)
my.amazing.model2 <- lmer(my.DV1 ~ cool.factor1 +
    cool.factor2 *
    cool.factor3 + (1|subject),
    data = my.amazing.data, REML=FALSE)
anova(my.amazing.model1,my.amazing.model2, refit=FALSE)
```

6.5.2. Logistic regression with random effects

When you are working with a binary dependent variable (e.g., "same" vs. "different" responses on a discrimination task), a logistic regression model can be used. Just as with linear regression, logistic regression models allow the inclusion of multiple independent variables that can be continuous, ordered, or discrete and that can be treated as main effects or involved in interactions with one another. While this type of test cannot be used to examine variation in responses to a dependent variable that has more than two levels, independent variables that are discrete can have any number of levels (assuming that they are appropriately represented in the data, see Section 6.2). This type of model is not appropriate when analyzing binary data that were not collected using multiple questions per participant (e.g., self-reported language attitudes where responses have been categorized as either negative or positive; instead see: chi-squared).

The syntax used to run a logistic regression model with random effects is almost identical to a linear model with random effects, with two changes: use "glmer" instead of "lmer" and add "family=binomial" to the end. All other code (e.g., adding interactions and random slopes) remains the same.

```
my.amazing.binary.model1 = glmer(my.DV2 ~ cool.factor1 +
    (1|subject), data=my.amazing.data, family=binomial)
summary(my.amazing.binary.model1)
```

When comparing the models, use the ANOVA-based methods outlined in Section 6.5.3 but replace the R syntax with that used for logistic regression models.

Interpreting the output from a logistic regression model is similar to a linear model except that, instead of working with predicted values of the dependent variable, we're working with the log odds of any given token being one factor level instead of the other.

Assuming you haven't releveled your data, this means that a positive estimated coefficient indicates a higher probability that a token will be whichever of your factors is alphabetically second. For example, if my dependent variable is coded as YES and NO, a positive estimated coefficient indicates an increase in the probability that the response will be YES. If you aren't sure or you feel it's more intuitive for the levels to be reversed, you can relevel your data:

```
my.amazing.data$DV2.
    releveled <- relevel(my.amazing.data$my.DV2,
    ref="YES")
```

After using the code above, a positive coefficient next to a factor indicates that the factor increases the likelihood of responding with whichever one is not the reference value specified in ref="". I generally find it more intuitive to have, when relevant, "NO" or "INCORRECT" as the reference value (so I wouldn't actually relevel my.amazing.data$my.DV2 like I've done here), but what is appropriate for you will depend on your data and your research question.

6.5.3. Ordered regression with random effects

Ordinal regression should be used when the dependent variable is a number (or could be ordered in some meaningful way) but it isn't actually continuous. For example, these types of models are an appropriate method for analyzing data collected from a rating task. Ordered regression models are a lot like linear regression models except that the dependent variable is not continuous, so there is an intercept for every interval between levels. For example, a study with three levels (agree-neutral-disagree) would have two intercepts (i.e., one between agree and neutral and one between neutral and disagree) and a study with five levels (strongly agree-agree-neutral-disagree-strongly disagree) would have four intercepts.

To step through how to fit an ordered regression model, we'll be treating cool.factor1 from the sample spreadsheet as the dependent variable. Before we can run the model, we need to make sure that R doesn't think the variable is continuous:

```
my.amazing.data$factor1.discrete <-
    as.factor(my.amazing.data$cool.factor1)
attach(my.amazing.data)
```

We also need to center the continuous fixed effect around the mean:

```
summary(my.amazing.data$my.DV1)
my.amazing.data$DV1rescaled <-
    scale(my.amazing.data$my.DV1, center=T, scale=T)
summary(my.amazing.data$DV1rescaled)
```

Before we can fit the model, we need to install and load the necessary package:

```
install.packages("ordinal")
library(ordinal)
```
Now we're ready to fit the model.
```
my.amazing.ordinal.model1 <- clmm(factor1.discrete ~
    DV1rescaled + (1|subject),
data = my.amazing.data)
summary(my.amazing.ordinal.model1)
```

The output for this type of model, shown in Figure 6.14, is a little bit different because it provides multiple intercepts, sometimes known as cutpoints. There is one cutpoint for every comparison between levels. The cutpoints are important in that they allow the model to avoid the assumption of continuity between the levels and meaningfulness of the intervals. However, the line that specifies the estimated coefficient is the most important for interpreting the results. This line is interpreted in the same way as it would be for linear regression.

6.6. The beloved p-value

Linguists (myself included) have relied heavily on *p*-values when interpreting results. But *p*-values are often misinterpreted. Contrary to popular belief, they do not provide information about confidence in the specific hypothesis being tested. Instead, they provide an indication of the confidence that the null hypothesis is false. The null hypothesis

Figure 6.14   An annotated example of output from an ordinal regression model

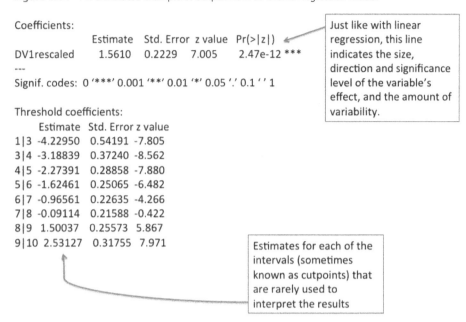

is that there is no difference between two populations, such as two conditions, that wouldn't just occur by chance. Thus, a small p-value indicates that it is likely that we would be correct in rejecting the null hypothesis. The direction and magnitude of the effect (found in the estimated coefficient column in the output of mixed effects models) and the amount of variation from this estimate (the standard deviation) are more informative than a p-value and should always be reported by the experimenter and considered by both the reader and the experimenter.

The inverse of assuming that small p-values indicate confidence in the specific hypothesis is assuming that larger p-values ($p>.05$) mean that there is no effect. More accurately, a researcher should say that they failed to find an effect. A failure to find an effect might be due to there not being one. Alternatively, it could be due to a number of other factors, such as not having a large enough number of tokens or participants (which together contribute to what is known in statistics as power).

6.7. Chapter summary

In this chapter, you have been introduced to R and have been shown how to produce graphs and conduct some statistical tests in R.

The introduction to R and statistics in this chapter is intended for those new to R and/or running inferential statistics. However, it's important to keep in mind that statistical tests are constantly being developed and improved upon. One advantage of working in R is that many of the people developing the tests also work in R, making it easier to stay on top of the latest and greatest methods for statistical analysis.

Once you feel comfortable with the content of this chapter, I recommend that you continue to develop your R and statistics knowledge. Some tests that I suspect you will find especially helpful in the analysis of your data are Generalized Additive Models (GAMMs), (fractional) polynomial regression, and inferential Bayesian statistics. Thus, I've included some references to tutorials on how to use some of these methods in the Further Reading section at the end of this chapter and some links to helpful tutorials on the companion website. You should also keep an eye out for a special issue on statistics, edited by Timo B. Roettger, Bodo Winter, and Harald Baayen, that is forthcoming in the *Journal of Phonetics*.

Main points

- Running statistics can be intimidating at first, but – once you learn how to do it and if you approach it as merely playing with your data – it can be a lot of fun.

- Whether you're plotting a graph or running a statistical model, it's important to know which tool is right for your data.

- Don't stop with what's covered in this chapter. Once you feel comfortable, seek out other resources to learn a wider range of skills and tests.

Further reading

Baayen, R. Harald (2008). *Analyzing Linguistic Data: A practical introduction to statistics using R.* Cambridge: Cambridge University Press.

Field, Andy, Jeremy Miles, and Zoë Field (2012). *Discovering Statistics Using R.* London: Sage. https://studysites.uk.sagepub.com/dsur/.

Hay, Jennifer (2011). Statistical analysis. In Marianna Di Paolo and Malcah Yaeger-Dror (Eds.) *Sociophonetics: A student guide.* London: Routledge, 198–214.

Johnson, Keith (2008). *Quantitative Methods in Linguistics.* London: Wiley-Blackwell.

Sóskuthy, M. (2017). Generalised additive mixed models for dynamic analysis in linguistics: A practical introduction. arXiv:1703.05339 [stat:AP]

Vasishth, Shravan and Bruno Nicenboim (2016). Statistical methods for linguistic research: Foundational ideas – Part I. *Language and Linguistics Compass* 10(8): 349–369, DOI: 10.1111/lnc3.12201.

Winter, B. (2013). Linear models and linear mixed effects models in R with linguistic applications. arXiv:1308.5499. http://arxiv.org/pdf/1308.5499.pdf.

Moving forward

7

Chapter outline

Go for it!

– Jennifer Hay (personal communication, many times)

In this book, we stepped through a variety of different experimental methods that have been used or could be used by sociolinguists. We also discussed an array of work focusing on vastly different research questions. Hopefully, you've learned some new methods or have figured out some ways you can improve your experimental research, and maybe you've even been inspired to ask research questions you hadn't thought of before. But even with the newfound knowledge and inspiration, you may not yet feel confident. *There is so much to think about, how do I know I'm ready?* The best way to gain confidence in your ability to set up and run experiments is to get out there and do it. I suggest starting with a pilot study and, during design and analysis, checking back with the book regularly to make sure that you remember all of the different aspects of setting up an experiment.

To aid in this endeavor, here is a checklist of some of the most important aspects of experimental design:

- My research question is specific.
- I have the necessary ethics training and approval to conduct the study.
- All factors that I'm interested in testing are balanced appropriately.
- I have controlled for all other factors that I think might affect the dependent variable, or they are appropriately balanced.
- My stimuli are counterbalanced.
- I have appropriate filler items.
- My stimuli are normed and, if resynthesized or modified in any way, I have conducted a test for naturalness.
- I have access to appropriate participants.

If you can tick every one of these boxes, you're ready to run your pilot experiment.

No, I'm stuck on the first one: my research question isn't specific or I don't know if it's specific enough. So how do I get started? How do I know when it's specific enough?

Read, read, read and – when you think you've read enough – read some more. This includes reading foundational studies and work that's only appeared recently. It may include reading outside the subfield if there is work that asks related questions or uses similar experimental paradigms. Sometimes it will feel like you're wasting your time because you won't cite every paper or book you read, but reassure yourself that this is a part of the process. Reading as much as possible will help lay the groundwork you need to ask the most interesting research questions and will help you to build knowledge about the methods you plan to use.

In determining what to read, I often start by working backwards. First, I identify a study with a research question that I find inspiring (perhaps by first encountering it while reading an overview like that in Chapter 1). After reading it (sometimes multiple times) and getting ideas for how it might be developed or modified, I read most if not all of the papers cited therein. For those that are most relevant, I then read the papers they cite, and so on. At the same time, I look for work that cites the original paper that I found so inspiring or that may be related in a way that is relevant to the direction I foresee taking the work in.

One of your goals in doing all of this background reading is to make sure that, by embarking on the path of following your research question, the work hasn't already been done by someone else. A second goal of all of this reading is to make sure that the research question you've identified or are in the process of identifying is specific enough. To do this, pay attention to the specific research question that is provided in the papers you read and, especially, in the paper that originally inspired you. How do you tweak it to make it relevant for the research you want to conduct? What are the broad questions of interest it is related to? Truthfully, it's hard to get too specific when running only a single experiment; the more you narrow it, the easier it will be to address certain questions that come up during experimental design.

A third reason for all of the reading is to make sure you aren't skipping steps between research questions. It may be tempting to ask a completely new and novel question, but unless the previous work naturally leads up to your current question, you'll need to do the work of building the steps to your ultimate research question. In addition to grounding your work, this is important because it makes it easier to interpret your results. Also, it can make it tricky to find an immediate audience for your work; working in increments helps build your audience naturally. If you're working too far ahead of the curve, your methods of data collection and analysis may well be obsolete by the time the rest of the field gets there, resulting in your work having a much smaller impact than if you'd been the one leading the field in that direction in the first place. So, by all means, think of novel and exciting studies to conduct and think of entirely new research questions, but do the work beforehand to identify how they connect with existing work and whether any steps are missing.

If you find that the steps don't yet exist, you can build them by replicating previous work and adding a twist. Adding a twist might entail running the experiment on a new dialect or changing something about the methods. Then, as you replicate your own experiments – adding more and more twists along the way – you can make your way toward answering the really cool and novel question that led you down this path in the first place. Plus, you might end up finding something new and cool that you weren't anticipating, and there's nothing wrong with that.

Once you have an idea for a research question, it gets easier and easier to determine which papers you should read, especially as the research question gets more and more specific. My favorite way to approach research is to have a hypothesis that tests some aspect of a theory and then seek out ways to prove the theory wrong during design and then try to prove myself wrong during analysis. (This is, in fact, how we came up with the idea for the stuffed toys study reported in Hay and Drager (2010). The theory predicted that we would see a result, but it was hard to believe we would.) During design, ask yourself "Is there anything else that could explain the expected result?" If the answer is "yes," then you should refine your design. Then during analysis, ask yourself "Could the results be explained by anything other than the factors being tested?" If the answer is "yes," then it becomes your job to measure and test those factors, if possible, or run a follow-up experiment to differentiate the different interpretations, if necessary. If neither is possible (immediately at least), then acknowledge the shortcoming in the manuscript where you report the results, taking care that you don't overstate your findings. At some point in the future, you can count on a reader spotting things you didn't think of (no matter how thorough you are), but being as thorough as possible from the beginning helps to decrease the number of critiques they can spot.

I really liked that method called X. Now I just have to figure out a research question to go with it!

This is not the right way to approach research. Just because a method sounds cool, fun, or interesting, that is not enough of a reason to pursue research that uses it. Let your research questions guide which methods you use, and you may find that you eventually end up with a research question that requires the use of one of those cool new-to-you methods.

However, if you are in a class that focuses on a single method and need to come up with an experiment that fits the requirements of the class, the best and most straightforward place to start is to select prior work that uses the method and then add your own twist.

Is there anything I should be reading other than work that uses similar methods or asks similar research questions?

It is critical that you stay current with the latest trends in statistical analysis. This usually means reading articles (or, better yet, attending workshops) by people outside your field, and especially those in fields that are highly quantitative and experimental. This is hard to do, but for quantitative sociolinguists who would like their work to impact linguistic theory and/or cognitive science more generally, it is critical that we put in the time and effort to stay up-to-date with the statistical methods considered standard in these areas.

The statistics presented in this book are just a starting point: there are many other options, some of which are increasingly being favored by experimentalists outside of sociolinguistics (see e.g., inferential Bayesian models). Once you master the basic skills outlined in Chapter 6, you'll be better prepared to tackle some of the up-and-coming methods.

I read the book and followed your instructions, but problems arose that I didn't anticipate. What do I do?

First, try to avoid the urge to throw your computer out the nearest window. Once you're calm, think about what you would do differently and be vocal about your mistakes so the rest of us can learn from them. All of us make mistakes and, in some cases, they can be enlightening and help push the field forward. Sharing our daftest moments (and even our less-daft-but-still-URGH!) moments can be difficult, especially for those of us who struggle with Imposter Syndrome, but it's important for the field so that others can learn from your mistakes. (Though it's completely understandable if you'd like to wait until you have job security to be vocal about your mistakes.)

7.1. Publishing replications and null results

It is critical that experimental work be replicated using methods highly similar to the original study. As mentioned in the preceding section, the most exciting way to approach replication studies is to replicate but add a twist. Including the twist will make it more exciting for you and will make it easier for you to publish the results, but it also has drawbacks. The biggest drawback is that – should you get a null result – you usually can't be sure whether it's due to a fault in the implementation or interpretation of the original study or to the change in the methods. (See e.g., Labov (1972), Blake & Josey (2003), and Pope, Meyerhoff, & Ladd 2007.) In addition, lags between data collection in the original study and a replication can be due to changes in the community, linguistic variable, or language variety that occurred in the interim, confounds that are relevant not only for sociolinguists but also for researchers working in experimental linguistics more generally.

Despite the difficulty in interpreting null results, null results are important for refining our theories. If the theory predicts that there should not be a null result given the method and language situation and a null result is observed nonetheless, the theory should be revisited and revised, or ditched altogether in favor of one that can account for the data. This is especially important given that we are still in the early stages of experimental work in sociolinguistics; we know that linguistic variables pattern with social factors in systematic and predictable ways, sometimes interacting with other linguistic variables, and we know that listeners have some degree of sensitivity to these associations during perception, but the exact nature of how this information is stored and processed is still up for debate. Much more work is needed – including null results in replication studies – to answer these questions.

Despite the advantages of publishing null results from sociolinguistic experiments, many journals and reviewers are reluctant to accept papers reporting null results. However, assuming the methods are sound and comparable to the original, replicated study, there needs to be some way for this work to appear so that we can use it to refine our theories.

7.2. Conclusion

Experimental methods can be used to answer many different research questions. Careful planning and attention to detail during the design are critical in experimental work. So plan the best you can, address any problems you can anticipate, and then jump in. After all, the best way to really learn the methods is to dive in and try them. *Go for it!*

Main points

- During experiment design, check back regularly until you feel comfortable and confident designing experiments.
- Don't skip steps in building your research program.
- Help others learn from your mistakes, warts and all.
- Replicate previous work, adding your own twist.
- Null results of replication studies deserve attention.

References

Adank, Patti and James M. McQueen (2007). The effect of an unfamiliar regional accent on spoken word comprehension. *Proceedings of the 16th International Congress of Phonetic Sciences*, Saarbrücken, 1925–1928. http://www.icphs2007.de/conference/Papers/1387/1387.pdf.

Addington, David W. (1968). The relationship of selected vocal characteristics to personality perception. *Speech Monographs* 35: 492–503.

Allopenna, Paul D., James S. Magnuson, and Michael K. Tanenhaus (1998). Tracking the time course of spoken word recognition using eye movements: Evidence for continuous mapping models. *Journal of Memory and Language* 38: 419–439.

Anderson, Anne H., Miles Bader, Ellen Gurman Bard, Elizabeth Boyle, Gwyneth Doherty, Simon Garrod, Stephen Isard, Jacqueline Kowtko, Jan McAllister, Jim Miller, Catherine Sotillo, Henry Thompson, and Regina Weinhart (1991). The HCRC Map task corpus. *Language and Speech* 34: 351–366.

Anderson, Anne, Gillian Brown, Richard Shillcock, and George Yule (1984). *Teaching Talk: Strategies for production and assessment.* Cambridge: Cambridge University Press.

Ash, Sharon (1988). Contextless vowel identification. Paper presented at NWAV XVII, Montreal.

Baayen, R. Harald (2008). *Analyzing linguistic data: A practical introduction to statistics using R.* Cambridge: Cambridge University Press.

Babel, Molly (2009). Phonetic and social selectivity in speech accommodation. Unpublished PhD dissertation, University of California, Berkeley.

Babel, Molly (2010). Dialect divergence and convergence in New Zealand English. *Language in Society* 39: 437–456.

Babel, Molly (2012). Evidence for phonetic and social selectivity in spontaneous phonetic imitation. *Journal of Phonetics* 40: 177–189.

Babel, Molly and Grant McGuire (2013). Listener expectation and gender bias in nonsibilant fricative perception. *Phonetica* 70: 117–151.

Babel, Molly and Jamie Russell (2015). Expectations and speech intelligibility. *Journal of the Acoustical Society of America* 137(5): 2823–2833.

Bailey, Guy and Natalie Maynor (1989). The divergence controversy. *American Speech* 64(1): 12–39.

Baker, Rachel E. and Ann R. Bradlow (2009). Variability in word duration as a function of probability, speech style, and prosody. *Language and Speech* 52(4): 391–413.

Baker, Rachel and Valerie Hazen (2011). DiapixUK: Task materials for the elicitation of multiple spontaneous speech dialogs. *Behavior Research Methods* 43: 761–770.

Ball, Peter and Howard Giles (1982). Speech style and employment selection: The matched guise technique. In Glynis M. Breakwell, Hugh Foot, and Robin Gilmour (Eds.) *Social Psychology: A practical manual.* London: The British Psychological Society, 101–121.

Balota, David A., Melvin J. Yap, Michael J. Cortese, Keith A. Hutchison, Brett Kessler, Bjorn Loftis, James H. Neely, Douglas L. Nelson, Greg B. Simpson, and Rebecca Treiman (2007). The English Lexicon Project. *Behavior Research Methods* 39: 445–459.

Baron-Cohen, Simon and Sally Wheelwright (2004). The empathy quotient: An investigation of adults with Asperger Syndrome or high functioning autism, and normal sex differences. *Journal of Autism and Developmental Disorders* 34(2): 163–175.

Barron-Lutzross, Auburn (2016). The production and perception of a lesbian speech style. Paper presented at the 15th Conference on Laboratory Phonology, Ithaca, New York.

Bayard, Donn (2000). The cultural cringe revisited: Changes through time in Kiwi attitudes toward accents. In Allan Bell and Koenraad Kuiper (Eds.) *New Zealand English.* Wellington: Victoria University Press, 297–324.

Bayley, Robert and Ceil Lucas (2007). *Sociolinguistic Variation: Theories, methods, and applications.* Cambridge: Cambridge University Press.

Beach, Elizabeth F., Denis Brunham, and Christine Kitamura (2001). Bilingualism and the relationship between perception and production: Greek/ English bilinguals and Thai bilabial stops. *International Journal of Bilingualism* 5(2): 221–235.

Becker, Kara (2013). The Sociolinguistic Interview. In Christine Mallinson, Becky Childs, and Gerard van Herk (Eds.) *Data Collection in Sociolinguistics.* London: Routledge, 91–100.

Becker, Michael and Jonathan Levine (2013). Experigen – an online experiment platform. Available at http://becker.phonologist.org/experigen.

Beckner, Clay, Péter Rácz, Jennifer Hay, Jürgen Brandstetter, and Christoph Bartneck (2016). Participants conform to humans but not to humanoid robots in an English past tense formation task. *Journal of Language and Social Psychology* 35(2): 158–179.

Bell, Allan (1984). Language style as audience design. *Language in Society* 13(2): 145–204.

Bergmann, Kirsten, Holly P. Branigan, and Stefan Kopp (2015). Exploring the alignment space – lexical and gestural alignment with real and virtual humans. *Frontiers in ICT* 2: 7. DOI: http://dx.doi.org/10.3389/ fict.2015.00007.

Blake, Renee and Meredith Josey (2003). The /ay/ diphthong in a Martha's Vineyard community: What can we say 40 years after Labov? *Language in Society* 32: 451–485.

Boyd, Zac, Zuzana Elliot, Josef Fruehwald, Lauren Hall-Lew, and Daniel Lawrence (2015). An evaluation of sociolinguistic elicitation methods. *Proceedings of the 18th International Congress of Phonetic Sciences.* Glasgow, UK: The University of Glasgow. ISBN 978-0-85261-941-4. Paper number 800. Retrieved from http://www.icphs2015.info/pdfs/Papers/ICPHS0800.pdf.

Brennan, Eileen M. and John S. Brennan (1981). Measurements of accent and attitude toward Mexican-American Speech. *Journal of Psycholinguistic Research* 10: 487–501.

van den Brink, Daniëlle, Jos J.A. Van Beerkum, Marcel C.M. Bastiaansen, Cathelijne M.J.Y. Tesink, Miriam Kos, Jan K. Buitlaar, and Peter Hagoort (2012). Empathy matters: ERP evidence for inter-individual differences in social language processing. *SCAN* 7: 173–183.

Brouwer, Susanne, Holger Mitterer, and Falk Huettig (2012). Can hearing puter activate pupil? Phonological competition and the processing of reduced spoken words in spontaneous conversations. *The Quarterly Journal of Experimental Psychology* 65: 2193–2220.

Brown-Schmidt, Sarah, Christine Gunlogson, and Michael K. Tanenhaus (2008). Addressees distinguish shared from private information when interpreting questions during interactive conversation. *Cognition* 107: 1122–1134.

Brunelle, Marc and Stefanie Jannedy (2013). The cross-dialect perception of Vietnamese tones: Indexicality and convergence. In Daniel Hole and Elizabeth Löbel (Eds.) *Linguistics of Vietnamese: An international survey*. Berlin/Boston: Mouton de Gruyter, 9–34.

Buchstaller, Isabelle (2006). Diagnostics of age-graded linguistic behavior: The case of the quotative system. *Journal of Sociolinguistics* 10(1): 3–10.

Buck, Joyce F. (1968). The effects of Negro and White dialectal variation upon attitudes of college students. *Speech Monographs* 35: 181–186.

Bush, Clara N. (1967). Some acoustic parameters of speech and their relationships to the perception of dialect differences. *TESOL Quarterly* 1: 20–30.

Butler, Joseph, Caroline Floccia, Jeremy Goslin, and Robin Panneton (2011). Infants' discrimination of familiar and unfamiliar accents in speech. *Infancy* 16(4): 392–417.

Camblin, C. Christine, Peter C. Gordon, and Tamara Y. Swaab (2007). The interplay of discourse congruence and lexical association during sentence processing: Evidence from ERPs and eye tracking. *Journal of Memory and Language* 56: 103–128.

Campbell-Kibler, Kathryn (2007). Accent, (ING), and the social logic of listener perceptions. *American Speech* 82(1): 32–64.

Campbell-Kibler, Kathyrn (2010a). The effect of speaker information on attitudes toward (ING). *Journal of Language and Social Psychology* 29(2): 214–223.

Campbell-Kibler, Kathryn (2010b). New directions in sociolinguistic cognition. *University of Pennsylvania Working Papers in Linguistics* 15(2): 31–39.

Campbell-Kibler, Kathryn (2011). Intersecting variables and perceived sexual orientation in men. *American Speech* 86(1): 52–68.

Campbell-Kibler, Kathryn (2012). The Implicit Association Test and sociolinguistic monitoring. *Lingua* 122: 753–763.

Chafe, Wallace L. (1980). *The Pear Stories: Cognitive, cultural, and linguistic aspects of narrative production*. Norwood, NJ: Ablex.

Chang, Charles (2008). Variation in palatal production in Buenos Aires Spanish. In Maurice Westmoreland and Juan Antonio Thomas (Eds.) *Selected Proceedings of the 4th Workshop on Spanish Sociolinguistics*. Somerville, MA: Cascadilla Proceedings Project, 54–63.

Chang, Yung-hsian Shawn (2015). Use of social information in the perception of Mandarin alveolar-retroflex contrast. *Proceedings of the 18th International Congress of the Phonetic Sciences*. London: International Phonetic

Association. https://www.internationalphoneticassociation.org/icphs-proceedings/ICPhS2015/Papers/ICPHS0589.pdf.

Cieri, Christopher (2011). Making a field recording. In Marianna Di Paolo and Malcah Yaeger-Dror (Eds.) *Sociophonetics: A student's guide*. Abingdon/New York: Routledge, 24–35.

Clark, Herbert H. and Deanna Wilkes-Gibbs (1986). Referring as a collaborative process. *Cognition* 22: 1–39.

Clarke, Constance M. and Merrill F. Garrett (2004). Rapid adaptation to foreign-accented English. *Journal of the Acoustical Society of America* 116(6): 3647–3658.

Clopper, Cynthia G. (2013). Experiments. In Christine Mallinson, Becky Childs, and Gerard Van Herk (Eds.) *Data Collection in Sociolinguistics: Methods and applications*. New York/London: Routledge, 151–161.

Clopper, Cynthia G. (2014). Sound change in the individual: Effects of exposure on cross-dialect speech processing. *Laboratory Phonology* 5(1): 69–90.

Clopper, Cynthia G., Janet B. Pierrehumbert, and Terrin N. Tamati (2010). Lexical neighborhoods and phonological confusability in cross-dialect word recognition in noise. *Laboratory Phonology* 1(1): 65–92.

Clopper, Cynthia G. and David B. Pisoni (2004). Homebodies and army brats: Some effects of early linguistic experience and residential history on dialect categorization. *Language Variation and Change* 16: 31–48.

Clopper, Cynthia G. and Terrin N. Tamati (2010). Lexical recognition memory across dialects. *The Journal of the Acoustical Society of America* 127(3): 1956. [abstract]

Cohn, Abigail C., Cécile Fougeron, and Marie K. Huffman (2012). *The Oxford Handbook of Laboratory Phonology*. Oxford: Oxford University Press.

Cooper, Roger M. (1974). The control of eye fixation by the meaning of spoken language: A new methodology for the real-time investigation of speech perception, memory, and language processing. *Cognitive Psychology* 6(1): 84–107.

Costa, Paul and Ignatius G. Mattingly (1981). Production and perception of phonetic contrast during phonetic change. *Journal of the Acoustical Society of America* 69: S67. [abstract] DOI: http://dx.doi.org.eres.library.manoa.hawaii.edu/10.1121/1.386167.

Csernicskó, István and Anna Fenyvesi (2012). Sociolinguistic and contact-induced variation in Hungarian language use in Subcarpathia, Ukraine. AHEA: E-journal of the American Hungarian Educators Association 3: 1–30. http://ahea.net/e-journal/volume-5-2012

Davidson, Lisa (2012). Ultrasound as a tool for speech research. In Abigail C. Cohn and Cécile Fougerson, and Marie K. Huffman (Eds.) *The Oxford Handbook of Laboratory Phonology*. Oxford: Oxford University Press, 484–496.

Davidson, Lisa and Paul De Decker (2005). Stabilization techniques for ultrasound imaging of speech articulations. *Journal of the Acoustical Society of America* 117(4): 2544. [abstract] DOI: http://dx.doi.org.eres.library.manoa.hawaii.edu/10.1121/1.4788460.

De Decker, Paul M. and Jennifer R. Nycz (2012). Are tense [æ]s really tense? The mapping between articulation and acoustics. *Lingua* 122: 810–821.

D'Onofrio, Annette (2015). Persona-based information shapes linguistic perception: Valley girls and California vowels. *Journal of Sociolinguistics* 19(2): 241–256.

Draegert, G.L. (1951). Relationships between voice variables and speech intelligibility in high level noise. *Communications Monographs* 18(4): 272–278.

Drager, Katie (2005). From bad to bed: The relationship between perceived age and vowel perception in New Zealand English. *Te Reo* 48: 55–68.

Drager, Katie (2011). Speaker age and vowel perception. *Language and Speech* 54(1): 99–121. DOI: 10.1177/0023830910388017.

Drager, Katie (2015). *Linguistic Variation, Identity Construction and Cognition.* Berlin: Language Science Press.

Drager, Katie, Jennifer Hay, and Abby Walker (2010). Pronounced rivalries: Attitudes and speech production. *Te Reo* 53: 27–53.

Drager, Katie and M. Joelle Kirtley (2016). Awareness, salience, and stereotypes in exemplar-based models of speech production and perception. In Anna Babel (Ed.) *Awareness and Control in Sociolinguistic Research.* Cambridge: Cambridge University Press, 1–24.

Drager, Katie, Rachel Schutz, Kate Hardeman Guthrie, and Ivan Chik (in prep). Perceptions of style: A focus on fundamental frequency and perceived social characteristics.

Dufour, Sophie, Angèle Brunellière, and Noël Nguyen (2013). To what extent do we hear phonemic contrasts in a non-native regional variety? Tracking the dynamics of perceptual processing with EEG. *Journal of Psycholinguistic Research* 42(2): 161–173.

Eckert, Penelope and Robert J. Podesva (2011). Sociophonetics and sexuality: Towards a symbiosis of sociolinguistics and laboratory phonology. *American Speech* 86(1): 6–13.

Edwards, Mary Louise (1974). Perception and production in child phonology: The testing of four hypotheses. *Journal of Child Language* 1(2): 205–219.

Elman, Jeffrey L., Randy L. Diehl, and Susan E. Buchwald (1977). Perceptual switching in bilinguals. *Journal of the Acoustical Society of America* 62(4): 971–974.

Epstein, Melissa A. (2005). Ultrasound and the IRB. *Clinical Linguistics and Phonetics* 19(6/7): 567–572.

Ervin-Tripp, Susan (1967). An Issei learns English. *Journal of Social Issues* 23(2): 78–90.

Evans, Bronwen G. and Paul Iverson (2007). Plasticity in vowel perception and production: A study of accent change in young adults. *Journal of the Acoustical Society of America* 121(6): 3814–3862.

Experiment [Def. 3]. (n.d.). In *Oxford English Dictionary*, Retrieved January 20, 2016, from online version via the University of Hawai'i library system.

Flanigan, Beverly Olson and Franklin Paul Norris (2000). Cross-dialectal comprehension as evidence for boundary mapping: Perceptions of the speech of southeastern Ohio. *Language Variation and Change* 12: 175–201.

Floccia, Caroline, Jeremy Goslin, Frédérique Girard, and Gabrielle Konopcznski (2006). Does a regional accent perturb speech processing? *Journal of Experimental Psychology* 32(5): 1276–1293.

Foulkes, Paul, Gerard Docherty, Ghada Khattab, and Malcah Yaeger-Dror (2010). Sound judgements: Perception of indexical features in children's speech. In Dennis R. Preston and N. Niedzielski (Eds.) *A Reader in Sociophonetics*. United States: De Gruyter Mouton, 327–356.

Freeman, Jonathan B. and Nalini Ambady (2010). MouseTracker: Software for studying real-time mental processing using a computer mouse-tracking method. *Behavior Research Methods* 42(1): 226–241. DOI: 10.3758/BRM.42.1.226.

Fridland, Valerie and Tyler Kendall (2012). Exploring the relationship between production and perception in the mid front vowels of U.S. English. *Lingua* 122: 779–793.

Fromont, Robert and Jennifer Hay (2012). LaBB-CAT: An annotation store. *Proceedings of the Australasian Language Technology Association Workshop*, Dunedin, 113–117.

Gao, Katie (2017). Dynamics of language contact in China: Ethnolinguistic diversity and variation in Wuding County, Yunnan. Unpublished PhD dissertation, University of Hawai'i at Mānoa. http://www.alta.asn.au/events/alta2012/proceedings/pdf/U12-1015.pdf

Gao, Katie B. and Nozomi Tanaka (2015). *The Cat Story: Wordless picture book*. Creative Commons Attribution-NonCommercial-ShareAlike 4.0 International License.

Gick, Bryan (2002). The use of ultrasound for linguistic phonetic fieldwork. *Journal of the International Phonetic Association* 32: 113–121. DOI: 10.1017/S0025100302001007.

Giles, Howard (1973). Accent mobility: A model and some data. *Anthropological Linguistics* 15: 87–105.

Giles, Howard and Peter F. Powesland (1975). *Speech style and social evaluation*. London: Academic Press.

Girard, Frédérique, Caroline Floccia, and Jeremy Goslin (2008). Perception and awareness of accents in young children. *British Journal of Developmental Psychology* 26: 409–433.

Gooskens, Charlotte, Wilbert Heeringa, and Karin Beijering (2008). Phonetic and lexical predictors of intelligibility. *International Journal of Humanities and Arts Computing* 2(1–2): 63–81.

Gorman, Kyle, Jonathan Howell, and Michael Wagner (2011). Prosodylab-Aligner: A tool for forced alignment of laboratory speech. *Canadian Acoustics* 39(3): 192–193.

Grama, James (2015). Variation and change in Hawai'i Creole vowels. Unpublished PhD dissertation, University of Hawai'i at Mānoa.

Green, Elizabeth J. and Paul J. Barber (1981). An auditory Stroop effect with judgments of speaker gender. *Perception and Psychophysics* 30(5): 459–466.

Greenwald, Anthony G., Debbie E. McGhee, and Jordan L.K. Schwartz (1998). Measuring individual differences in implicit cognition: The Implicit Association Test. *Journal of Personality and Social Psychology* 74(6): 1464–1480.

Greenwald, Anthony G., Brian A. Nosek, and Mahsarin R. Banaji (2003). Understanding and using the Implicit Association Test: I. An improved scoring algorithm. *Attitudes and Social Cognition* 85(2): 197–216.

Greenwald, Anthony G., T. Andrew Poelman, Eric Luis Uhlmann, and Mahzarin R. Banaji (2009). Understanding and using the Implicit Association Test: III. Meta-analysis of predictive validity. *Journal of Personality and Social Psychology* 97(1): 17–41.

Gross, Johan, Sally Boyd, Therese Leinonen, and James A. Walker (2016). A tale of two cities (and one vowel): Sociolinguistic variation in Swedish. *Language Variation and Change* 28: 225–247.

Hall-Lew, Lauren and Bartlomiej Plichta (2013). Technological challenges in sociolinguistic data collection. In Christine Mallinson, Becky Childs, and Gerard Van Herk (Eds.) *Data Collection in Sociolinguistics: Methods and applications*. London/New York: Routledge, 127–130.

Hanna, Joy E., Michael K. Tanenhaus, and John C. Trueswell (2003). The effects of common ground and perspective on domains of referential interpretation. *Journal of Memory and Language* 49: 43–61.

Hardeman Guthrie, Kate (2013). Gender and Second Language Style: American learner perception and use of Mandarin *sajiao*. Unpublished PhD dissertation, University of Hawai'i at Mānoa.

Hardeman Guthrie, Kate (2016). Gender and second language style: American learner perceptions of Mandarin *sajiao*. *Asia Pacific Language Variation* 2(2): 157–187.

Harnsberger, James D., Richard Wright, and David B. Pisoni (2008). A new method for eliciting three speaking styles in the laboratory. *Speech Communication* 50(4): 323–336.

Hasty, J. Daniel (2015). Well, he may could have sounded nicer: Perceptions of the double modal in doctor-patient interactions. *American Speech* 90(3): 347–368.

Hay, Jennifer and Katie Drager (2007). Sociophonetics. *Annual Review of Anthropology* 36: 89–103.

Hay, Jennifer and Katie Drager (2010). Stuffed toys and speech perception. *Linguistics* 48(4): 865–892.

Hay, Jennifer, Katie Drager, and Andy Gibson (forthcoming). Hearing /r/-sandhi: The role of past experience. To appear in *Language*.

Hay, Jennifer, Katie Drager, and Paul Warren (2009). Careful who you talk to: An effect of experimenter identity on the production of the NEAR/SQUARE merger in New Zealand English. *Australian Journal of Linguistics* 29(2): 269–285.

Hay, Jennifer, Katie Drager, and Paul Warren (2010). Short-term exposure to one dialect affects processing of another. *Language and Speech* 53(4): 447–471.

Hay, Jennifer, Aaron Nolan, and Katie Drager (2006a). From fush to feesh: Exemplar priming in speech perception. *The Linguistic Review* 23: 351–379.

Hay, Jennifer, Paul Warren, and Katie Drager (2006b). Factors influencing speech perception in the context of a merger-in-progress. *Journal of Phonetics* 34(4): 458–484.

Hay, Jennifer, Stefanie Jannedy, and Norma Mendoza-Denton (1999). Oprah and /ay/: Lexical frequency, referee design and style. In John J. Ohala, Yoko Hasegawa, ManjariOhala, Daniel Granville, and Ashlee C. Bailey (Eds.)

Proceedings of the 14th International Congress of Phonetic Sciences, 1389–1392. San Francisco: University of California.

Hazen, Kirk (2014). A historical assessment of research questions in sociolinguistics. In Janet Holmes and Kirk Hazen (Eds.) *Research Methods in Sociolinguistics: A practical guide*. Malden, MA: Wiley-Blackwell, 7–22.

Hehman, Eric, Ryan M. Stolier, and Jonathan B. Freeman (2014). Advanced mouse-tracking analytic techniques for enhancing psychological science. *Group Processes and Intergroup Relations* 18(3): 1–18. DOI: 10.1177/1368430214538325.

Hellmuth, Sam (2005). No de-accenting in (or of) phrases: Evidence from Arabic for cross-linguistic and cross-dialectal prosodic variation. In Sónia Frota, Marina Vigário, and Maria João Freitas (Eds.) *Prosodies: With special reference to Iberian languages*. Berlin/New York: Mouton de Gruyter, 99–121.

Hellmuth, Sam (2014). Dialectal variation in Arabic intonation: Motivations for a multi-level corpus approach. In Samira Farwaneh and Hamid Ouali (Eds.) *Perspectives on Arabic Linguistics XXV-XXVI*. Philadelphia/Amsterdam: John Benjamins, 63–89.

Hesson, Ashley and Madeline Shellgren (2015). Discourse marker *like* in real time: Characterizing the time-course of sociolinguistic impression formation. *American Speech* 90(2): 154–186.

Higgins, Christina (2003). "Ownership" of English in the outer circle: An alternative to the NS-NNS Dictionary. *TESOL Quarterly* 37(4): 615–644.

Hill, Joseph (2013). Special issues in collecting interview data for sign language projects. In Christine Mallinson, Becky Childs, and Gerard Van Herk (Eds.) *Data Collection in Sociolinguistics: Methods and applications*. New York/London: Routledge, 110–113.

Hilton, Nanna Haug and Charlotte Gooskens (2013). Language policies and attitudes towards Frisian in the Netherlands. In Charlotte Gooskens and Renee van Bezooijen (Eds.) *Phonetics in Europe: Perception and production*. Frankfurt am Main: Peter Lang, 139–157.

Hilton, Nanna Haug, Charlotte Gooskens, and Anja Schüppert (2013). The influence of non-native morphosyntax on the intelligibility of a closely related language. *Lingua* 137: 1–18.

Hoffman, Michol (2014). Sociolinguistic interviews. In Janet Holmes and Kirk Hazen (Eds.) *Research Methods in Sociolinguistics*. Malden, MA: Wiley-Blackwell, 25–41.

Huettig, Falk and James M. McQueen (2007). The tug of war between phonological, semantic and shape information in language-mediated visual search. *Journal of Memory and Language* 57: 460–482.

Huettig, Falk, Joost Rommers, and Antje S. Meyer (2011). Using the visual world paradigm to study language processing: A review and critical evaluation. *Acta Psychologica* 137(2): 151–171.

Hurley, Robert S., Molly Losh, Morgan Parlier, J. Steven Reznick, and Joseph Piven (2007). The Broad Autism Phenotype Questionnaire. *Journal of Autism Development Disorders* 37: 1679–1690.

Hwang, Heeju and Elsi Kaiser (2014). The role of the verb in grammatical function assignment in English and Korean. *Journal of Experimental Psychology: Learning, Memory, and Cognition* 40(5): 1363–1376.

Idemaru, Kaori, Bodo Winter, and Lucien Brown (2015). The role of pitch in perceiving politeness in Korean. *Proceedings of the 18th International Congress of the Phonetic Sciences.* London: International Phonetic Association. https://www.internationalphoneticassociation.org/icphs-proceedings/ICPhS2015/Papers/ICPHS0214.pdf.

Jacewicz, Ewa and Robert Allen Fox (2012). The effects of cross-generational and cross-dialectal variation on vowel identification and classification. *Journal of the Acoustical Society of America* 131(2): 1413–1433.

Janson, Tore and Richard Schulman (1983). Non-distinctive features and their use, *Journal of Linguistics* 19: 321–336.

Jeon, Lisa and Patricia Cukor-Avila (2015). "One country, one language"?: Mapping perceptions of dialects in South Korea. *Dialectologia* 14: 17–46.

Johnson, Keith, Elizabeth A. Strand, and Mariapaola D'Imperio (1999). Auditory-visual integration of talker gender in vowel perception. *Journal of Phonetics* 27: 359–384.

Johnstone, Barbara (2000). *Qualitative Methods in Sociolinguistics.* Oxford: Oxford University Press.

Kamide, Yuki, Gerry T.M. Altmann, and Sarah L. Haywood (2003). The time-course of prediction in incremental sentence processing: Evidence from anticipatory eye movements. *Journal of Memory and Language* 49: 133–156.

Kendall, Tyler and Erik R. Thomas (2010). Vowels: Vowel manipulation, normalization, and plotting in R. R package. cran.r-project.org/web/packages/vowels/index.html.

Kerswill, Paul (2001). A dialect with "great inner strength"? The perception of nativeness in the Bergen speech community. *Reading Working Papers in Linguistics* 5: 23–49.

Kim, Jonny (2016). Perceptual associations between words and speaker age. *Laboratory Phonology* 7(1): 1–22. DOI: http://dx.doi.org/10.5334/labphon.33.

Kim, Midam, William S. Horton, and Ann R. Bradlow (2011). Phonetic convergence in spontaneous conversations as a function of interlocutor language distance. *Laboratory Phonology* 2: 125–156. DOI: 10.1515/LABPHON.2011.004.

Kim, Mi-Ryoung (2014). Ongoing sound change in the stop system of Korean: A three- to two-way categorization. *Studies in Phonetics, Phonology and Morphology* 20(1): 51–82.

Kinzler, Katherine D. and Jasmine M. DeJesus (2013). Northern = smart and Southern = nice: The development of accent attitudes in the United States. *The Quarterly Journal of Experimental Psychology* 66(6): 1146–1158.

Khattab, Ghada and Julie Roberts (2010). Working with children. In Marianna Di Paolo and Malcah Yaeger-Dror (Eds.) *Sociophonetics: A student's guide.* Abingdon/New York: Routledge, 163–178.

Kirtley, M. Joelle (2015). Language, identity, and non-binary gender in Hawai'i. Unpublished PhD dissertation, University of Hawai'i at Mānoa, December 2015.

Koops, Christian (2011). Local sociophonetic knowledge in speech perception. Unpublished PhD dissertation, Rice University.

Koops, Christian, Elizabeth Gentry, and Andrew Pantos (2008). The effect of perceived speaker age on the perception of PIN and PEN vowels in Houston,

Texas. *University of Pennsylvania Working Papers in Linguistics: Selected Papers from NWAV 36*, 14: 93–101.

Kraljic, Tanya and Arthur G. Samuel (2011). Perceptual learning evidence for contextually-specific representations. *Cognition* 121: 459–465.

Kristiansen, Tore (2009). The macro-level social meanings of late-modern Danish accents. *Acta Linguistica Hafniensia* 41: 167–192.

Labov, William (1966). *The Social Stratification of English in New York City*. Washington D.C.: Center for Applied Linguistics.

Labov, William (1972). *Sociolinguistic Patterns*. Philadelphia: University of Pennsylvania Press.

Labov, William (2001). *Principles of Linguistic Change, vol. 1: Internal factors*. Oxford: Blackwell.

Labov, William (2010). *Principles of Linguistic Change, vol. 3: Cognitive and cultural factors*. Oxford: Wiley-Blackwell.

Labov, William (2012). What is to be learned? The community as the focus of social cognition. *Review of Cognitive Linguistics* 10(2): 265–293.

Labov, William and Sharon Ash (1997). Understanding Birmingham. In Cynthia Bernstein, Thomas Nannally, and Robin Sabino (Eds.) *Language Variety in the South Revisited*. Tuscaloosa: University of Alabama Press.

Labov, William, Sharon Ash, and Charles Boberg (2005). *The Atlas of North American English: Phonetics, phonology, and sound change*. Berlin/New York: Mouton de Gruyter.

Labov, William, Sharon Ash, Maya Ravindranath, Tracey Weldon, and Naomi Nagy (2011). Properties of the sociolinguistic monitor. *Journal of Sociolinguistics* 15(4): 431–463.

Labov, William, Mark Karen, and Coery Miller (1991). Near-mergers and the suspension of phonemic contrast. *Language Variation and Change* 3: 33–74.

Labov, William, Malcah Yaeger, and Richard Steiner (1972). *A Quantitative Study of Sound Change in Progress*. Report on National Science Foundation Contract NSF-GS-3287.

Ladefoged, Peter and D.E. Broadbent (1957). Information conveyed by vowels. *Journal of the Acoustical Society of America* 29(1): 98–104.

Lambert, W.E., R.C. Hodgson, R.C. Gardner, and S. Fillenbaum (1960). Evaluational reactions to spoken languages. *Journal of Abnormal and Social Psychology* 60(1): 44–51.

Lawrence, Daniel (2015). Limited evidence for social priming in the perception of the BATH and STRUT vowels. *Proceedings of the 18th International Congress of the Phonetic Sciences*. Glasgow, London: International Phonetic Association. https://www.internationalphoneticassociation.org/icphs-proceedings/ICPhS2015/Papers/ICPHS0244.pdf.

Lawson, Eleanor, James M. Scobbie, and Jane Stuart-Smith (2011). The social stratification of tongue shape for postvocalic /r/ in Scottish English. *Journal of Sociolinguistics* 15(2): 256–268.

Lawson, Eleanor, Jane Stuart-Smith, and James M. Scobbie (2014). A mimicry study of adaptation towards socially-salient tongue shape variants. *University of Pennsylvania Working Papers in Linguistics: Selected Papers from NWAV 42*, 20(2): 101–110.

Lev-Ari, Shiri and Boaz Keysar (2010). Why don't we believe non-native speakers? The influence of accent on credibility. *Journal of Experimental Social Psychology* 46: 1093–1096.

Levon, Erez (2007). Sexuality in context: Variation and the sociolinguistic perception of identity. *Language in Society* 36: 533–554.

Levon, Erez (2014). Categories, stereotypes, and the linguistic perception of sexuality. *Language in Society* 43: 539–566.

Levon, Erez and Isabelle Buchstaller (2015). Perception, cognition, and linguistic structure: The effect of linguistic modularity and cognitive style on sociolinguistic processing. *Language Variation and Change* 27: 319–348.

Likert, Rensis (1932). A technique for the measurement of attitudes. *Archives of Psychology* 22: 5–55.

Lipski, John M. (2011). Socio-phonological variation in Latin American Spanish. In Manuel Díaz-Campos (Ed.) *The Handbook of Hispanic Sociolinguistics*, Malden, MA: Wiley-Blackwell,72–97.

Lipski, John M. (2014). Syncretic discourse markers in Kichwa-influenced Spanish: Transfer vs. emergence. *Lingua* 151: 216–239.

Llamas, Carmen and Dominic Watt (2014). Scottish, English, British?: Innovations in attitude measurement. *Language and Linguistics Compass* 8(11): 610–617.

Llamas, Carmen, Dominic Watt, and Daniel Ezra Johnson (2009). Linguistic accommodation and the salience of national identity markers in a border town. *Journal of Language and Social Psychology* 28: 381–407. DOI: 10.1177/ 0261927X09341962.

Llamas, Carmen, Dominic Watt, and Andrew E. MacFarlane (2016). Estimating the relative sociolinguistic salience of segmental variables in a dialect boundary zone. *Frontiers in Psychology* 7(1163): 1–18. DOI:10.3389/fpsyg.2016.01163.

Llompart and Miquel Simonet (forthcoming). Unstressed vowel reduction across Majorcan Catalan dialects: Production and spoken word recognition. To appear in Language and Speech.

Lombard, E. (1911). Le signe de l'elevation de la voix. *Annales des Maladies d l'Oreille, du Larynx, du Nez et du Pharynx* 37: 101–119. [used 2006 translation by Paul H. Mason].

Loudermilk, Brandon C. (2015). Implicit attitudes and the perception of sociolinguistic variation. In Alexei Prikhodkine and Dennis R. Preston (Eds.) *Responses to Language Varieties: Variability, processes and outcomes.* Philadelphia/Amsterdam: John Benjamins, 137–156. DOI: 10.1075/ impact.39.06lou.

Love, Jessica and Abby Walker (2012). Football versus football: Effect of topic on /r/ realization in American and English sports fans. *Language and Speech* 56(4): 443–460.

Luck, Steven J. (2014). *An Introduction to the Event-Related Potential Technique*, 2nd edition. Cambridge, MA: MIT Press.

Mack, Sara and Benjamin Munson (2012). The influence of /s/ quality on ratings of men's sexual orientation: Explicit and implicit measures of the 'gay lisp' stereotype. *Journal of Phonetics* 40: 198–212.

Maclagan, Margaret and Jennifer Hay (2011). Transcription. In Marianna Di Paolo and Malcah Yaeger-Dror (Eds.) *Sociophonetics: A student's guide*, Abingdon/New York: Routledge, 36–45. http://lib.ugent.be/catalog/ rug01:001447937

Mallinson, Christine, Becky Childs, and Gerard Van Herk (2013). *Data Collection in Sociolinguistics: Methods and applications.* New York/ London: Routledge.

McCarthy, Owen and Jane Stuart-Smith (2013). Ejectives in Scottish English: A social perspective. *Journal of the International Phonetic Association* 43(3): 273–298.

McGowan, Kevin (2011). The role of socioindexical expectation in speech perception. Unpublished PhD dissertation, University of Michigan.

McGowan, Kevin B. (2015). Social expectation improves speech perception in noise. *Language and Speech*, 1–20. DOI: 10.1177/0023830914565191.

McGuire, Grant and Molly Babel (2015). Facial attractiveness facilitates voice processing. *Proceedings of the 18th International Congress of the Phonetic Sciences*. Glasgow, London: International Phonetic Association. https://www.internationalphoneticassociation.org/icphs-proceedings/ICPhS2015/Papers/ICPHS0812.pdf.

Mendoza-Denton, Norma, Jennifer Hay, and Stefanie Jannedy (2003). Probabilistic sociolinguistics: Beyond variable rules. In Rens Bod, Jennifer Hay, and Stefanie Jannedy (Eds.), *Probabilistic Linguistics*, Cambridge, MA: MIT Press, 97–138.

Most, Steven B., Anne Verbeck Sorber, and Joseph G. Cunningham (2007). Auditory Stroop reveals implicit gender associations in adults and children. *Journal of Experimental Social Psychology* 43: 287–294.

Munson, Benjamin (2011). The influence of actual and imputed talker gender on fricative perception, revisited. *Journal of the Acoustical Society of America* 130(5): 2631–2634.

Munson, Benjamin and Molly Babel (2007). Loose lips and silver tongues, or, projecting sexual orientation through speech. *Language and Linguistics Compass* 1: 416–449.

Munson, Benjamin, Sarah V. Jefferson, and Elizabeth C. McDonald (2006). The influence of perceived sexual orientation on fricative identification. *Journal of the Acoustical Society of America* 119(4): 2427–2437.

Munson, Benjamin, Elizabeth C. McDonald, Nancy L. DeBoe, and Aubrey R. White (2006). The acoustic and perceptual bases of judgments of women and men's sexual orientation from read speech. *Journal of Phonetics* 34: 202–240.

Natale, Michael (1975). Convergence of mean vocal intensity in dyadic communication as a function of social desirability. *Journal of Personality and Social Psychology* 32: 790–804.

Nathan, Liz, Bill Wells, and Chris Donlan (1998). Children's comprehension of unfamiliar regional accents: A preliminary investigation. *Journal of Child Language* 25: 343–365.

Niedzielski, Nancy (1999). The effect of social information on the perception of sociolinguistic variables. *Journal of Language and Social Psychology* 18: 62–85.

On Yoon, Si and Sarah Brown-Schmidt (2014). Adjusting conceptual pacts in three-party conversation. *Journal of Experimental Psychology: Learning, Memory, and Cognition* 40(4): 919–937.

Pantos, Andrew J. and Andrew W. Perkins (2012). Measuring implicit and explicit attitudes toward foreign accented speech. *Journal of Language and Social Psychology* 32(1): 3–20.

Patterson, Michelle L. and Janet F. Werker (2002). Infants' ability to match dynamic information in the face and voice. *Journal of Experimental Child Psychology* 81: 93–115.

Pardo, Jennifer S. (2006). On phonetic convergence during conversational interaction. *Journal of the Acoustical Society of America* 119(4): 2382–2393.

Pardo, Jennifer S. (2012). Reflections on phonetic convergence: Speech perception does not mirror speech production. *Language and Linguistics Compass* 6(12): 753–767.

Pharao, Nicolai, Marie Maegaard, Janus Spindler Møller, and Tore Kristiansen (2014). Indexical meanings of [s+] among Copenhagen youth: Social perception of a phonetic variant in different prosodic contexts. *Language in Society* 43: 1–31.

Pichler, Heike (2016). *Discourse-Pragmatic Variation and Change in English: New Methods and Insights*. Cambridge, UK: Cambridge University Press.

Plichta, Bartlomiej and Dennis R. Preston (2005). The /ay/s have it: The perception of /ay/ as a north-south stereotype in United States English. *Acta Linguistica Hafniensia* 37(1): 107–130.

Podesva, Robert J. (2007). Phonation type as a stylistic variable: The use of falsetto in constructing a persona. *Journal of Sociolinguistics* 11(4): 478–504.

Pope, Jennifer, Miriam Meyerhoff, and D. Robert Ladd (2007). Forty years of language change on Martha's Vineyard. *Language* 83(3): 615–627.

Post, Brechtje and Francis Nolan (2012). Data collection for prosodic analysis of continuous speech and dialectal variation. In Abigail C. Cohn, Cécile Fougeron, and Marie K. Huffman (Eds.) *The Oxford Handbook of Laboratory Phonology*. Oxford: Oxford University Press, 538–547.

Preston, Dennis R. (1996). Where the worst English is spoken. In Edgar Schneider (Ed.) *Focus on the USA*, Amsterdam: John Benjamins, 297–360.

Preston, Dennis R. (1999). *Handbook of Perceptual Dialectology*. Amsterdam/Philadelphia: John Benjamins.

Purnell, Thomas, William Idsardi, and John Baugh (1999). Perceptual and phonetic experiments on American English dialect identification. *Journal of Language and Social Psychology*, 18(1): 10–30. DOI: 10.1177/0261927X99018001002.

Rau, Victoria D. (2013). Cross-cultural issues in studying endangered indigenous languages. In Christine Mallinson, Becky Childs, and Gerard Van Herk (Eds.) *Data Collection in Sociolinguistics: Methods and applications*. New York/London: Routledge, 101–104.

Ravindranath, Maya (2015). Sociolinguistic variation and language contact. *Language and Linguistics Compass* 9(6): 243–255.

Reddy, Sravana and James Stanford (2015). Toward completely automated vowel extraction: Introducing DARLA. *Linguistics Vanguard* 1(1): 15–28. DOI: https://doi.org/10.1515/lingvan-2015-0002.

Rickford, John R. and Faye McNair-Knox (1994). Addressee- and topic-influenced style shift: A quantitative sociolinguistic study. In Douglas Biber and Edward Finegan (Eds.) *Sociolinguistic Perspectives on Register*. Oxford: Oxford University Press, 235–276.

Riverin-Coutlée, Josiane and Vincent Arnaud (2015). Regional backgrounds and discrimination patterns: A preliminary perceptual study in Quebec French. *Proceedings of the 18th International Congress of the Phonetic Sciences*. London: International Phonetic Association. https://www.internationalphoneticassociation.org/icphs-proceedings/ICPhS2015/Papers/ICPHS0625.pdf.

Rosenfelder, Ingrid, Josef Fruehwald, Keelan Evanini, Scott Seyfarth, Kyle Gorman, Hilary Prichard, and Jiahong Yuan (2014). FAVE (Forced Alignment and Vowel Extraction) Program Suite v1.2.2 10.5281/ zenodo.22281.

Rosseel, Laura, Dirk Speelman, and Dirk Geeraerts (2015). Can social psychological attitude measures be used to study language attitudes? A case study exploring the Personalized Implicit Association Test. In Johannes Wahle, Marisa Köllner, HaraldBaayen, Gerhard Jäger, and TinekeBaayen-Oudshoorn (Eds.) *Proceedings of the 6th Conference on Quantitative Investigations in Theoretical Linguistics*, Tübingen, 1–4.

Rubin, Donald L. (1992). Nonlanguage factors affecting undergraduates' judgments of nonnative English-speaking teaching assistants. *Research in Higher Education* 33(4): 511–531.

Scarborough, Rebecca, Jason Brenier, Yuan Zhao, Lauren Hall-Lew, and Olga Dmitrieva (2007). An acoustic study of real and imagined foreigner-directed speech. *Proceedings of ICPhS XVI*, Saarbrücken, 2165–2168. http://icphs2007.de/conference/Papers/1673/1673.pdf.

Schafer, Amy J., Shari R. Speer, and Paul Warren (2005). Prosodic influences on the production and comprehension of syntactic ambiguity in a game-based conversation task. In M. Tanenhaus and J. Trueswell (Eds.) *Approaches to Studying World Situated Language Use: Psycholinguistic, Linguistic and Computational Perspectives on Bridging the Product and Action Tradition.* Cambridge, MA: MIT Press, 209–225.

Schnoebelen, Tyler and Katie Drager (2014). The perception of social types: Using LDA to analyze open-response answers. Paper presented at the International Conference on Language and Social Psychology 14. Honolulu, June 2014.

Schüppert, Anja, Nanna Haug Hilton, and Charlotte Gooskens (2015). Swedish is beautiful, Danish is ugly? Investigating the link between language attitudes and spoken word recognition, *Linguistics* 53(2): 375–403.

Scobbie, James M. and Jane Stuart-Smith (2012). Socially-stratified sampling in laboratory-based phonological experimentation. In Abigail C. Cohn, Cécile Fougeron, and Marie K. Huffman (Eds.) *The Oxford Handbook of Laboratory Phonology*. Oxford: Oxford University Press, 607–621.

Scobbie, James M., Jane Stuart-Smith, and Eleanor Lawson (2008). Looking variation and change in the mouth: Developing the sociolinguistic potential of Ultrasound Tongue Imaging. Unpublished Research Report for ESRC Project RES-000-22-2032. Downloaded December 13, 2016 from https://core.ac.uk/download/pdf/41504.pdf.

Sharma, Devyani (2011). Style repertoire and social change in British Asian English. *Journal of Sociolinguistics* 15(4): 464–492.

Sheldon, Amy and Winifred Strange (1982). The acquisition of /r/ and /l/ by Japanese learners of English: Evidence that speech production can precede speech perception. *Applied Psycholinguistics* 3(3): 243–261.

Sloetjes, Han and Peter Wittenburg (2008). Annotation by category – ELAN and ISO DCR. *Proceedings of the 6th International Conference on Language Resources and Evaluation* (LREC 2008). Developed at: The Max Planck Institute for Psycholinguistics, The Language Archive, Nijmegen, The Netherlands. http://tla.mpi.nl/tools/tla-tools/elan/

Speelman, Dirk, Adriaan Spruyt, Leen Impe, and Dirk Geeraerts (2013). Language attitudes revisited: Auditory affective priming. *Journal of Pragmatics* 52: 83–92.

Squires, Lauren (2013a). Talker specificity and the perception of grammatical variation. *Language and Cognitive Processes* 21(1). DOI: 10.1080/01690965.2013.804193.

Squires, Lauren (2013b). It don't go both ways: Limited bidirectionality in sociolinguistic perception. *Journal of Sociolinguistics* 17(2): 200–237.

Squires, Lauren (2014). Processing, evaluation, knowledge: Testing the perception of English subject-verb agreement variation. *Journal of English Linguistics* 42(4): 144–172.

Stamp, Rose (2016). Do signers understand regional varieties of a sign language? A lexical recognition experiment. *Journal of Deaf Studies and Deaf Education* 21(1): 83–93.

Stamp, Rose, Adam Schembri, Bronwen G. Evans, and Kearsy Cormier (2016). Regional sign language varieties in contact: Investigating patterns of accommodation. *Journal of Deaf Studies and Deaf Education* 21(1): 70–83.

Stanford, James N. (2010). Gender, generations, and nations: An experiment in Hmong American discourse and sociophonetics. *Language and Communication* 30: 285–296.

Staum Casasanto, Laura (2008). Does social information influence sentence processing? *Proceedings of the 30th Annual Meeting of the Cognitive Science Society*. Washington, D.C: Cognitive Science Society.

Staum Casasanto, Laura, Kyle Jasmin, and Daniel Casasanto (2010). Virtually accommodating: Speech rate accommodation to a virtual interlocutor. In Stellan Ohlsson and Richard Catrambone (Eds.) *Proceedings of the 32nd Annual Conference of the Cognitive Science Society*. Austin, TX: Cognitive Science Society, 127–132.

Strand, Elizabeth (1999). Uncovering the role of gender stereotypes in speech perception. *Journal of Language and Social Psychology* 18: 86–99.

Strand, Elizabeth and Keith Johnson (1996). Gradient and visual speaker normalization in the perception of fricatives. In Dafydd Gibbon (Ed.) *Natural Language Processing and Speech Technology*, 14–26. Berlin: Mouton de Gruyter.

Stroop, J. Ridley (1935 [reprint1992]). Studies of interference in serial verbal reactions. *Journal of Experimental Psychology* 18: 643–662.

Sumner, Meghan and Arthur G. Samuel (2009). The effect of experience on the perception and representation of dialect variants. *Journal of Memory and Language* 60: 487–501.

Swerts, Marc, Emiel Krahmer, and Cinzia Avesani (2002). Prosodic marking of information status in Dutch and Italian: A comparative analysis. *Journal of Phonetics* 30: 629–654.

Szakay, Anita (2008). *Ethnic Dialect Identification in New Zealand: The role of prosodic cues*. Saarbrücken: VDM Verlag.

Szakay, Anita (2012). Voice quality as a marker of ethnicity in New Zealand: From acoustics to perception. *Journal of Sociolinguistics* 16(3): 382–397.

Szakay, Anita, Molly Babel, and Jeanette King (2016). Social categories are shared across bilinguals' lexicons. *Journal of Phonetics* 59: 92–109.

Szmrecsanyi, Benedikt (2005). Language users as creatures of habit: A corpus-based analysis of persistence in spoken English. *Corpus Linguistics & Linguistic Theory* 1(1): 113–150.

Tanenhaus, Michael K., Michael J. Spivey-Knowlton, Kathleen M. Eberhard, and Julie C. Sedivy (1995). Integration of visual and linguistic information in spoken language comprehension. *Science* 268: 1632–1634.

Tanenhaus, Michael K. and John C. Trueswell (2006). Eye movements and spoken language comprehension. In Matthew J. Traxler and Morton A. Gernsbacher (Eds.) *Handbook of Psycholinguistics,* 2nd edition. Amsterdam/Boston: Elsevier, 863–900.

Thakerar, Jitendra N. and Howard Giles (1981). They are – so they spoke: Noncontent speech stereotypes. *Language and Communication* 1(2/3): 255–261.

Thomas, Erik (2002). Sociophonetic applications of speech perception experiments. *American Speech* 77(2): 115–147.

Thomas, Erik R. (2011). *Sociophonetics: An introduction.* Basingstoke: Palgrave Macmillan.

Thomas, Erik and Jeffrey Reaser (2004). Delimiting perceptual cues used for the ethnic labeling of African American and European American voices. *Journal of Sociolinguistics* 8: 54–87.

Trude, Alison M. and Sarah Brown-Schmidt (2012). Talker-specific perceptual adaptation during online speech perception. *Language and Cognitive Processes* 27(7/8): 979–1001. DOI: 10.1080/01690965.2011.597153.

Tucker, Richard G. and Wallace E. Lambert (1969). White and Negro listeners' reactions to various American-English dialects. *Social Forces* 47: 463–468.

Van Berkum, Jos J.A., Daniëlle van den Brink, Cathelijne M.J.Y. Tesink, Miriam Kos, and Peter Hargoort (2008). The neural integration of speaker and message, *Journal of Cognitive Neuroscience* 20(4): 580–591.

Van Engan, Kristin J., Melissa Bease-Berk, Rachel E. Baker, Arim Choi, Midam Kim, and Ann R. Bradlow (2010). The Wildcat Corpus of native- and foreign-accented English: Communicative efficiency across conversational dyads with varying language alignment profiles. *Language and Speech* 53(4): 510–540. DOI: 10.1177/0023830910372495.

Varon, Sara (2007). *Robot Dreams.* New York: First Second.

Vitevitch, Michael S., Joan Sereno, Allard Jongman, and Rutherford Goldstein (2013). Speaker sex influences processing of grammatical gender. *PLoS ONE* 8(11): e79701. DOI: 10.1371/ journal.pone.0079701.

Wagner, Laura, Cynthia Clopper, and John K. Pate (2014). Children's perception of dialect variation. *Journal of Child Language* 41: 1062–1084.

Wagner, Suzanne Evans and Hesson, Ashley (2014). Individual sensitivity to the frequency of socially meaningful linguistic cues affects language attitudes. *Journal of Language and Social Psychology* 33(6): 651–666.

Walker, Abby (2008). The effect of phonetic detail on the grammaticality judgements given to variable morpho-syntactic constructions in New Zealand English. Unpublished MA thesis, University of Canterbury.

Walker, Abby and Kathryn Campbell-Kibler (2015). Repeat after whom? Exploring variable selectivity in a cross-dialectal shadowing task. *Frontiers in Psychology* 6(546): 1–18. DOI: 10.3389/fpsyg.2015.00546.

Walker, Abby, Christina García, Yomi Cortés, and Kathyrn Campbell-Kibler (2014). Comparing social meanings across listener and speaker groups: The indexical field of Spanish /r/. *Language Variation and Change* 26: 169–189.

Walker, Abby and Jennifer Hay (2011). Congruence between 'word age' and 'voice age' facilitates lexical access. *Laboratory Phonology* 2(1): 219–237.

Walker, Michael S. (2016). Regional priming in Australian KIT, DRESS and TRAP vowels. Unpublished MRe thesis, Macquarie University.

Warren, Paul (2014). Sociophonetic and prosodic influences on judgments of sentence types. In Jennifer Hay and Emma Parnell (Eds.) *Proceedings of the 15th Australasian International Conference on Speech Science and Technology.* Christchurch: ASSTA, 185–188.

Warren, Paul and Jennifer Hay (2012). Methods and experimental design for studying sociophonetic variation, In Abigail C. Cohn, Cécile Fougeron, and Marie K. Huffman (Eds.) *The Oxford Handbook of Laboratory Phonology.* Oxford: Oxford University Press, 634–642.

Watson, Kevin and Lynn Clark (2015). Exploring listeners' real-time reactions to regional accents. *Language Awareness* 24(1): 38–59.

Wells, William D. and Geogianna Smith (1960). Four semantic rating scales compared. *Journal of Applied Psychology* 44(6): 393–397.

Wheelwright, S, S. Baron-Cohen, Nigel Goldenfeld, Joe Delandy, Debra Fine, Richard Smith, Leonora Weil, and Akio Wakabayashi (2006). Predicting Autism Spectrum Quotient (AQ) from the Systemizing Quotient-Revised (SQ-R) and Empathy Quotient (EQ). *Brain Research* 1079: 47–56.

Williams, Angie, Peter Garrett, Nikolas Coupland (1999). Dialect recognition. In Dennis R. Preston (Ed.) *Handbook of Perceptual Dialectology.* Philadelphia: John Benjamins, 345–358.

Willis, Erik W. and Travis G. Bradley (2008). Contrast maintenance of taps and trills in Dominican Spanish: Data and analysis. In Laura Colantoni and Jeffrey Steele (Eds.) *Selected Proceedings of the Third Conference on Laboratory Approaches to Spanish Phonology.* Somerville, MA: Cascadilla Press, 87–100.

Wolff, Hans (1959). Intelligibility and inter-ethnic attitudes. *Anthropological Linguistics* 1(3): 34–41.

Yonezawa Morris, Midori (1999). Regional stereotypes and the perception of Japanese vowel devoicing. In Dennis R. Preston and Nancy Niedzielski (Eds.) *Trends in Linguistics. Studies in Monographs [TiLSM]: A reader in sociophonetics*, Berlin/Boston: De Gruyter Mouton, 191–202.

Yoon, Si On and Sarah Brown-Schmidt (2014). Adjusting conceptual pacts in three-party conversation. *Journal of Experimental Psychology: Learning, Memory, and Cognition* 40(4): 919–937.

Yu, Alan C.L. (2010). Perceptual compensation is correlated with individuals' "autistic" traits: Implications for models of sound change. *PLoS ONE* 5(8): 1–9. DOI:10.1371/journal.pone.0011950.

Yu, Alan C.L., Carissa Abrego-Collier, and Morgan Sonderegger (2013). Phonetic imitation from an individual-difference perspective: Subjective attitude, personality, and "autistic" traits. *PLoS ONE* 8(9): 1–13. DOI:10.1371/journal.pone.0074746.

Yu, Alan C.L. and Hyunjung Lee (2014). The stability of perceptual compensation for coarticulation within and across individuals: A cross-validation study. *Journal of the Acoustical Society of America* 136(1): 382–388.

Zimman, Lal (2013). Hegemonic masculinity and the variability of gay-sounding speech: The perceived sexuality of transgender men. *Journal of Language and Sexuality* 2(1): 1–39.

Index